Metatheater

Judd D. Hubert

METATHEATER

The Example of Shakespeare

University of Nebraska Press
Lincoln & London

Manufactured in the United States of America
The paper in this book
meets the minimum
requirements of American National Standard
for Information Sciences—
Permanence of Paper for
Printed Library Materials,
ANSI Z39.48–1984.

Library of Congress Cataloging-in-Publication Data
Hubert, Judd David, 1917–
Metatheater : the example of Shakespeare /
Judd D. Hubert.
p.   cm.
Includes bibliographical references (p.)
and index.
ISBN 0-8032-2355-2 (cl)
1. Shakespeare, William, 1564–1616—Technique.
I. Title. PR2995.H84   1991
822.3′3—dc20
90–22718
CIP

Portions of the following chapters have previously
been published in different form: Chapter 4 as
"The Textual Presence of Staging and Acting in
Measure for Measure,"
New Literary History 18 (Spring 1987): 583–96;
Chapter 5 as "*Othello* ou les récits de la traîtrise,"
Silex 26 (1984): 47–56; and Chapter 6 as
"Hamlet, Student Prince and Actor,"
in *The Dialectic of Discovery: Essays
on the Teaching and Interpretation of
Literature Presented to Lawrence E. Harvey,*
ed. John D. Lyons and Nancy J. Vickers,
French Forum Monographs 50
(Lexington, Ky.: French Forum, 1984), 132–44.

To Candice

CONTENTS

Que devient, ou que redevient,

ce verbe nul, ce verbe ETRE, qui

a fait une si grande carrière

dans le vide?

What will become, or what will become once more,
of that useless verb "to be," which
carved out so great a career for itself
in the void.

Paul Valéry

ONE

Metatheater and Performance

This study features a performative as opposed to a mimetic approach, based to a large extent on emphasizing linguistic signs that, in addition to communicating developments in plot and characterization, explicitly or implicitly designate the art of stagecraft and entertainment. These signs serve a metaphorical purpose insofar as they transfer or transport elements involving content to performative schemes ascribable to the medium. It does not really matter, for the present purpose, if some of these signs happen to assume additional metaphorical or metonymic functions within the context of the fable. When Macbeth states: "The Thane of Cawdor lives. Why do you dress me / In borrowed robes?" (I.iii.108–9), his words, from the standpoint of the unfolding plot, relate to an impending usurpation of rank while metaphorically evoking costuming as a preliminary to performance.[1] Macbeth implies that Ross wishes to dress him for a part preempted by another. My particular use of the term "performative" requires further clarification, particularly because I look for performative indications within the text instead of deriving them from stagings by famous directors—from actual performances in the concrete sense of the term. In any case, I could hardly use "performative" in any but a metaphorical sense, for I intend to show how the medium operates, by means of latent comparisons, away from, though not necessarily in opposition to, mimetic representation, which paradoxically relies on staging. This standoff relationship between mimesis and performance could lead to a division of scholarly labors or even to a parting of the ways: the more critics focus on the fable, the more they tend to concern themselves with the accuracy of the play's representation of a reality outside the theater. It does of course matter whether they have merely studied the text or actually seen the play performed, for in the first instance they can legitimately judge the verisimilitude of plot and characterization in terms of what they consider real and authentic, and in the second they can in addition legislate on how well each performer has understood and lived up to his or her part and determine to what extent the director has remained faithful to the script. The search for performative clues, on the contrary, takes place within an imaginary space where mimetic reconstructions of the fable give way to the operations involved in overdetermining spectacle and entertainment, henceforth perceived as cause rather than result. Moreover, a performative approach need not limit itself to a discussion of metadrama in a limited sense—to the self-designation of theater as theater. In *Much Ado about Nothing,* for instance, performative insights frequently arise from country dancing and counterpoint rather than from specifically metadramatic awareness, while in *Twelfth Night* they originate in the verbal performances displayed in poetic interpenetration.

Theater constantly produces double images by combining overt mimetic representations of the story with covert performative and metadramatic clues pointing to its own operations at the risk of undermining or at the very least of problematizing the fable. In *King Lear* Edmund's aside upon his brother's entrance provides a fairly obvious example of this kind of maneuver: "and pat he comes, like the catastrophe of the old comedy. My cue is villainous melancholy, with a sigh like Tom o' Bedlam" (I.ii.130–32). Edgar will fittingly extirpate himself from the villain's plot by playing with appropriate sighs the part of Tom o' Bedlam. Thus will poetic justice prevail. Paradoxically, this kind of device, however contrived, insincere, and artificial it may appear, far from ruining the emotional impact of a tragedy, frequently serves to enhance its most intense moments, whereas the recounted event, however fascinating as a story, might have only a minimal effect without an overdetermination of the medium—of theatrical machinery. As spectators, we need never suspend our disbelief, because all along we consciously indulge in, and react to, patently fabricated fictions. In this connection, the suffering of Lear moves us all the more because at the end of the tragedy he willy-nilly joins the spectators in the capacity of chief and designated witness of his own undoing, as Edgar's final summation, situating both the dead King and himself within the audience, appears to show: "The oldest hath borne most; we that are young—Shall never see so much, nor live so long" (V.iii.326–27). In this particular instance, a self-referential theatrical image intensifies and brings artistic closure to the story. Such meta-dramatic exchanges between protagonist and audience appear to encourage in the latter a more active participation; and perhaps identification with a character can occur only when we as spectators burden ourselves with some of the performative responsibilities of the cast. In this particular instance, we attempt to shoulder the tremendous weight that the aged king can no longer bear. As the unobtrusive parallel expressions "see so much" and "live so long" in no way function as metaphors within the overt content of the scene, it follows that their metaphoricity depends solely on a transfer or displacement from stage to audience: the final step in King Lear's programmed descent from his initial position of power as dramatist and director. After serving as reluctant performer in the evil scenarios of others and acting out his insanity, he ends his long life as a pathetic spectator, whose lack of impact on the action contributes to the overwhelming effect he produces on the offstage audience.

Although such metaphorical readings of Shakespeare's scripts owe much to contextualism, deconstructive strategies—Burkean even more than Derridian—have led to the treatment of plays as performative scores rather than self-sufficient texts by stressing the transfers or, better still, the displacements between mimesis on the one hand and self-referentiality and performance on the other. Kenneth Burke's dramatistic method pervades the entire essay. He has examined the relationships among such fundamental notions as act, scene, agent, agency, and purpose and has shown how deceptively they can lend themselves to permutation. Not only has he unmasked unstated displacements and reversals as well as other hidden maneuvers at work in various types of seemingly "innocent" discourse, but he has revealed the complexities involved in ascribing purposes and motives. Since action prevails over knowledge in a dramatistic approach, it applies perfectly to performative displacement in drama.[2]

Displacement, a term reiterated throughout the book, designates whatever metaphorical transfers, switches, and reversals may serve to bring into the limelight the performative scheme of the play. While pretending that drama functions in the manner of a self-centered, lucid, and ruthlessly aggressive agent, acutely aware of its every move, I have made room for deconstructive strategies by entrusting each play with the responsibility of unraveling both itself and its referential others as well as theater in general. Thus, the obvious "as if" clauses in my approach originate in, imitate, and repeat theatricality. By centering power within the literary masterpiece, my method obviously differs from that of the "new historicists," who fruitfully seek sources of potency in the historical context and, so to speak, in the referential others of works of art.[3] As the purpose of this book consists in focusing on various crucial aspects of metatheater and performative metaphor rather than in making informative contributions to Shakespearean studies, it addresses itself primarily to readers concerned with the problematics and aesthetics of theatricality and secondarily to specialists, who may, despite their acquaintance with all aspects of Shakespearean drama, nevertheless find the application of performative metaphor to drama useful. I have chosen to write about Shakespeare mainly because his productions allow for the exploration of just about every aspect of theatrical representation.

The aesthetic bias given to deconstructive strategies and the attempt to bridge the gap between seemingly incompatible approaches and positions have no doubt left me in an exposed situation, midway between a "new criticism" shorn of organicism and an unorthodox offshoot of poststructuralism. My high regard for postulates, covert as well as overt, placed at the cutting edge of intellectual pursuits insofar as they can lead to the bracketing for productive purposes of previously acquired apprehensions of the "truth," may have unduly complicated the fairly straightforward interpretive task of assessing some of Shakespeare's contributions to the art of entertaining an audience. After all, the proof of a theory's or of a method's value in normative disciplines such as literary criticism lies in the relevance of its results or at least in the beneficial shock the latter may produce rather than in premises and promises. I feel in many respects like those eighteenth-century French wits called upon to pen elaborate prefaces which they expected, and sometimes advised, their readers to skip. Conversely, nothing has prevented some of today's most prominent theoreticians from publishing book-length, self-contained, self-sufficient, and obviously indispensable prefaces.

The interpretive success of deconstruction, particularly among American poststructural critics such as J. Hillis Miller, results mainly from innovative postulates, capable of providing in one way or another the dynamic reversal of apparent negativity into positive insight.[4] Indeed, deconstruction, in spite of or by reason of its very name and title, frequently evolves from an incisive philosophical pursuit into elaborate and aesthetically meaningful literary constructs. Other and no less relevant poststructural concepts such as dispersion, difference, displacement, trace, and supplement, have promoted similar changes and reversals. Nonetheless, difference, whatever its spelling, may repress, but can scarcely eliminate, analogy, always ready to burst upon the scene at the slightest provocation and, at the very least, prove its usefulness in literary analysis.[5] It would seem, moreover, that difference and different, both of them negative and hence relative or complementary concepts insofar as they imply their unmentioned opposite, resemblance, entail recognition and hence analogy. The unstated persistence of analogy becomes clearer if we substitute for "different" the frequently synonymous and even more explicitly negative term "unlike." While "different" and "analogous," or "unlike" and "like," would seem to refer to, and polarize, one and the same operation, it would appear that "different" as compared with "unlike," by substituting for and, so to speak, unseating and displacing analogy, at least in Saussurian linguistics, has the distinct advantage of keeping metaphors in abeyance while surreptitiously making full use of their potentialities. Such reversals or permutations should hardly surprise us, for in negation language and rhetoric may have achieved some of their greatest poetic triumphs but without coming any closer to the "truth," as Henri Bergson has so clearly demonstrated.[6] In any case, the reinstatement of analogy as a spaced-out adjunct of "difference" might prove helpful in the aesthetic application of deconstructive strategies to dramatic works, no longer perceived as self-sufficient organic wholes but nevertheless as coherent and cohesive verbal constructs set up in opposition to the world outside and, at privileged moments, for the latter's pleasurable entrapment.

By means of the muted *a* in *différance,* Derrida introduces a deferral in time. According to Eric Partridge's *Origins,* deferring in the sense of postponing actually provides the etymological background of "difference," so we can say that "difference" already contains by virtue of its etymology a few of the temporal implications of "différance" and thus involves postponement, suspension, and perhaps even suspense as a deferral of the outcome.[7] Patricia Parker has shown the relevance of Derridean *différance* to the study of Shakespeare by associating it with the concept of dilation: "*Dilate* comes to us from the same Latin root as Derrida's *différance* and involves—commonly throughout Renaissance usage in several languages—that term's curious combination of difference and deferral, dilation, expansion, or dispersal in space, but also postponement in time."[8] The concepts of "different" and "unlike" would thus have even less in common than previously intimated, for "unlike" does not overtly or even covertly refer to postponement. For that matter, such antonyms as "like" and "analogous" have little to do with simultaneity. The manipulation of time, particularly in the sense of deferral or expansion, may play as seminal a part in theatrical displacement—particularly in *Othello* and *The Winter's Tale*—as in deconstruction itself. Finally, metaphorical displacement from content to performance involves *différance* and "dilation," for it entails the setting up of intervals between meaning and function, between plot and performance.[9]

In dealing with a literary work, deconstructionists can hardly avoid approaching it from two distinct and separate chronological stances, both of them a deliberate step removed from an artistic present and presence. They project the work into an expanding future as *écriture,* while simultaneously relegating it to a past—to an imaginary instant immediately preceding its production, at which moment it remains indeterminate and undecidable because of the many dispersive forces and potentialities actively engaged.[10] The operation of *différance* may thus mark a strategic and perfectly controlled return to that bipolar operation of the mind which, according to Bergson, gives rise to the arrogations of both determinism and free will.[11] For practical purposes, I have attempted to situate this dual operation within the performative script itself, perceived in terms of possible openings and closures in the performance though not in referential discourse. Moreover, deconstructive strategies may not apply in quite the same way to plays as to other kinds of writing, for we can only partially reduce a dramatic score, whose "truth" emerges in performance, to *écriture*. In spite of a common recourse to rhetorical devices, a theatrical approach departs from a deconstructive one insofar as the former treats the text as a performative score, while the latter concerns itself mainly with generating textuality. In short, a performative study shows deference, in both senses of the word, to rhetorical deconstruction in order to pay even greater homage to theatricality.

The printed text of a play functions as a performative score demanding in its every word, sign, image, and metaphor immediate staging in the presence of an audience. A constant performative thrust informs and subverts the various significata of the script, however profoundly and movingly the latter may affect the reader or spectator from a moral, psychological, or metaphysical standpoint. In short, my analysis of a dramatic text will consist mainly if not exclusively in a search for performative clues, such as the only too obvious indications provided in Edmund's aside—in a search for metadramatic stage directions and manipulations so often imbedded in the most gripping dialogues and soliloquies. A working hypothesis, assumption, rule of thumb, formula, recipe—call it what you will—underlies my performative and metadramatic approaches to all dramatic scripts. I have formulated this heuristic hypothesis axiomatically: A psychological or moral determination in a character invariably coincides with his or her performative failure or success as dramatist, director, player, spectator. It follows that the theater, in order to ensure its triumphs, tends to substitute its own peculiar set of professional values for those prevailing, if not in the outside world, at least within the expectations of an audience; and thus the stage expresses to a fault strengths or weaknesses deemed universal while covertly and sometimes overtly reasserting its own generic imperatives. In short, theater features a subversive power game leading to entrapment—a game played exclusively for the pleasure, sometimes masochistic, of an apprehensive but appreciative audience. Hamlet's famous Mousetrap might serve in this respect as a symbol for all theater, always prone to catch the consciousness if not the conscience of its intended audience.

Macbeth provides, however, a far more compelling model of performative failure than does the prince of Denmark, who displays on so many occasions unusual mastery of the stage. The usurper fails as actor, for not only does he find the crown and royal robes of Scotland far too big for him, but in crucial circumstances he does not know how to cast himself in, and perform, a suitable part.[12] He fails also as dramatist and director, for in his every move he requires the promptings of the witches or of his wife. Finally, he fails as critical spectator, for, unlike Banquo, he takes at face value the deceptive show staged for his undoing by three untrustworthy hags. A skilled actor entrusted with this demanding role would obviously know how to take full advantage of the protagonist's numerous performative lapses. Macbeth's various failures in performance correspond to, and transfer into theatrical terms, ambition, usurpation, unworthiness, cruelty, and indecision, all of them crucial to the understanding of character and the unfolding of the plot or, in other words, to a persuasive recounting of the story, to a plausible fictional narrative of the events.

Only a few tragic protagonists, Lear among them, actually fail performatively in as many ways as Macbeth. Oedipus, the paragon of all tragic heroes, guilty perhaps of the sin of hubris, succumbs because his merely human scenario can hardly match the protracted plotting of the gods, but as actor he successfully rises to the occasion in all his appearances both as king and as victim.[13] Unlike Sophocles, Corneille, eager to stage the heroic tribulations of human enterprise and reason, insists on the spectacular failure of the gods, whose cowardly behavior and repugnant manipulations cannot compare with Oedipe's purely human prowess, particularly his heroically self-inflicted blindness, which allows him to stage a final performance capable of upstaging Apollo together with all his myths and oracles.[14] In any case, dramatists, at least those of the past, require some sort of performative failure on the part of their morally questionable characters or actants, even when the latter shamefully hide themselves from public view. In comedy, on the contrary, the hero or heroine can on occasion achieve complete performative mastery. Isabelle in Molière's *Ecole des maris* so cleverly directs and coaches Sganarelle that her perfectly planned scenario very nearly backfires when her obedient tyrant gleefully insists, as a special favor to her, on advancing the hour scheduled for their wedding. In *Volpone,* Mosca shows even greater theatrical skills than Isabelle, but his plan fails in the end because by accelerating too rapidly it completely escapes his control. Petruchio in *The Taming of the Shrew* achieves definitive performative victories in dealing, not with a mechanical stooge and an assortment of gulls, but with an intelligent and imaginative woman who may have discovered in excessive obedience the best technique for taming her domineering husband.

Because of this deliberate focusing on performative means at the expense of mimesis and a tendency to perceive performance as cause rather than as result, my conception of a play may no longer conform to Webster's definition: "The representation or exhibition of some action or story on the stage." I therefore propose for the time being an alternative that happens to suit my project. I define a play, from a performative standpoint, as a fugal interplay between illusion and elusion.[15] While "playing" makes its presence felt not only in "interplay," but also, by etymology (*ludere,* in "illusion" and "elusion") "story" remains somewhat in abeyance by reason of its reduction to make-believe and evasion. Illusion, similar in some respects to Patricia Parker's concept of "dilation," refers to the positive, if at times playful, building up and unfolding of plot and characterization, while elusion designates such negative or unraveling aspects of dramatic unfolding as a character's explicit or implicit reluctance to perform the part assigned by the author. Without elusion, *Hamlet, Prince of Denmark* might hardly have outlasted the first act; and Racine's *Phèdre* might never have reached the stage if we take into account Hippolyte's intent to leave Trézène and the name character's unwillingness to enter the scene. Elusion in these two tragedies rises of course to unprecedented heights, because the built-in tension between the author, who enforces casting, and his characters, who must willy-nilly accept his dictates, could scarcely go much further. Characters usually fit more graciously if not more gracefully, though rarely without some resentment, into their assigned roles, and seldom do they rebel against their creator—never of course without express permission to question his paternal authority. In a way, a character's reluctance to play a part provides a measure of the purely illusory and elusory freedom deliberately if only hypocritically foisted on them by the dramatist.

The term "fugal" in my definition relates theater to the playing of music, particularly music of the contrapuntal sort prevalent in Shakespeare's, Corneille's, Molière's, and Racine's time. And music as metaphor may key us into some of the salient performative aspects of *Much Ado about Nothing* and *Twelfth Night*. By means of the fugal interplay between illusion and elusion, a play unravels in the very act of building itself up. This double movement constantly at work during the chronological unfolding of a drama gives rise to suspended time, definable as a period of inaction during which the play continues nonetheless to pursue its relentless but dilatory course toward a conclusion. One of the most successful tragedies of the French Renaissance, Jean de La Taille's *Saül le Furieux* (1572), a play that Shakespeare may very well have read, features more clearly perhaps than any other work of the period suspended time and deliberate inertness.[16] While the king's sons dutifully build up illusion in their active preparations for war against the Philistines, Saül in the throes of madness continues to enthrall the audience during his vain but highly eloquent search for the causes of God's silence. Although he performatively dominates the play from beginning to end, he never contributes positively to the events, but destroys instead whatever his sons have done their utmost to accomplish. Far from participating in the action of the play, he eludes all involvement and functions only in suspended time, the time of his insanity and of God's silence. The actual war against the Philistines occupies no more than a few scattered scenes and narratives serving as preambles to, and as aftermath of, Saül's compelling performance. King Lear, his mind even more stormy than that of Saül, functions during most of the tragedy in suspended time. It would thus seem that elusion reaches a climax , if not in insanity as such, at least in the protagonist's inability to focus on events. Suspended time, in less extreme forms, appears in every play worthy of the name, for illusion as a purely linear chronological development lacks both the matter and the energy to sustain itself on its own. For obvious reasons, *Hamlet* provides a remarkably structured example of the use of elusion and suspended time.

In insisting on performance, illusion, elusion I have conveniently mimimized or upstaged the so-called content of a play. I do not deny, however, the importance of persuasive plots, of psychological motivation that appears true to life, of a playwright's all-encompassing humanity, of his or her visionary and prophetic grasp of truth. After all, many people go to the theater not only for casual entertainment but also with the expectation of deepening or at least confirming their knowledge of the human condition; and Shakespeare may very well have deserved all the praise that advocates of his intellectual superiority have traditionally heaped upon him. Actually, I have conveniently bracketed content and mimesis in order to focus on Shakespeare's dramatic genius and discover in his plays revealing aspects of playwriting.

While the study of the fable definitely contributes to an understanding of theater even in its performative aspects, as Aristotle so clearly showed in the very first recorded graduate seminar on literary theory, we can hardly take the plot for granted, for, no less than performance, it poses complex critical problems. Try as we may, we can never isolate content by separating it either from its abstract other, form, or its concrete other, referentiality. Content in drama presupposes indeed a concatenation of referents outside the literary work that presumably guarantee its faithfulness to reality, whether psychological, sociological, or historical. In praising a play for realism and authenticity, we fall back on our experience, little realizing that experience itself consists of a complex kind of memory, capable of combining knowledge acquired from past events or readings with the recent impact of a stage performance. But, as everybody knows, the staging or even the reading of a play can induce in all of us an irresistible impression of authenticity that we generously if at times misguidedly attribute to content.

Magritte's famous painting *This Is Not a Pipe* has relevance to theatrical representation in the sense that a play may venture so far in the direction of realism as to represent a "true" event but will never come close to coinciding with it. At the other extreme, a play dealing with pure fantasy can do no less than generate its own referent, while pretending all along to reproduce it. But art has no greater foe than reality, taken in the sense of everyday existence. The world around us makes art works so frail and vulnerable that they have to resort to a considerable amount of trickery merely to survive, and they pretend to imitate reality in order to assert themselves through the manipulation and even the imagined destruction of their overwhelming other. Negation and deprivation in lyric poetry, violence in the novel and in drama, provide three of the most frequently used and effective devices enabling literature to hold its own against the inroads of daily existence. And perhaps performance, far from conforming to a referent outside itself, provides the best means for capturing, subordinating, and finally sacrificing the everyday world for the sake of artistic triumph. I realize that such aesthetic imperatives or, worse still, imperialism may strike not only new historicists but even a few deconstructionists as elitist heresy.

I have chosen for performative commentary three comedies: *Twelfth Night, Much Ado about Nothing,* and *Measure for Measure*; two tragedies: *Othello* and *Hamlet*; and a single romance, *The Winter's Tale.* Such a selection may strike the reader as arbitrary; and indeed other plays might have served a similar if not necessarily better metadramatic and performative purpose. But then any other selection might have struck the reader as no less arbitrary. In any case, I have deliberately chosen works as different from one another as possible, each one exemplifying a distinct implementation of metatheater and a unique distribution of performative clues. While *Twelfth Night* appears essentially lighthearted and festive, *Much Ado about Nothing* features somber moments and thrives at times on cruelty. That most puzzling of comedies, *Measure for Measure,* though by no means classifiable as a romance, borders nevertheless on tragicomedy. Nor can we consider the two tragedies generically untainted, for *Hamlet* abounds in displays of wit, while *Othello,* unmistakably tragic, frequently relies on techniques pertaining to, if not borrowed from, low comedy.[17] The first half of *The Winter's Tale* affords the audience very few occasions for laughter, whereas the second part combines scenes of farce and pastoral, leading to the spectacular but generically undefinable staging that closes the romance. In short, the six works I have selected may suffice to reveal salient and differing aspects of theatricality from the standpoint of genre and content.

Differentiation in these two respects did not, however, provide as compelling a reason for including or excluding a play as its performative uniqueness. Even in systematically overdetermining performative aspects, I have not consciously taken into account the specific interpretation, staging, and direction of compelling productions by eminent directors such as Peter Brooks. As I have already suggested, I must forgo this undoubtedly fruitful dramaturgic approach in favor of metaphorical clues presumably located within the script. I realize that this approach to theatrical performance, by relying too heavily on close readings of scripts, may regrettably appear too literary to appeal to stage people actively engaged in production. In fact, precise performative readings by such eminent Shakespearean scholars as Maurice Charney, Inga-Stina Ewbank, R. A. Foakes, and Ann Pasternak Slater might more readily or more overtly serve their professional needs than metaphorical indirection.[18]

In *Much Ado about Nothing,* I stress the rhetorical intrusions throughout the play of such nonverbal spectacles as music and dancing, which reduce dramatic reversals and motives to dizzy permutations. Indeed, psychological verisimilitude does not matter in the least, and characters can completely change their attitude and behavior from one scene to the next as though their director had unaccountably instructed them to play completely different parts.

Twelfth Night, though considered for good reasons Shakespeare's most festive play, paradoxically multiplies exclusions, divisions, and frames, a technique that would seem to militate against the carnivalesque rejoicings promised by the title and repeated in so many scenes. But then, every masterpiece of the stage undergoes in its unfolding opposing movements reminiscent of tides and revealing fugal interplay. Verbal interpenetration, lyrical and euphuistic as well as farcical, contributes to the breaking down and sometimes even to the erection or maintenance of these barriers.

Metadramatic devices gain the upper hand in *Measure for Measure,* which features in Vincentio a political leader who by effectively performing as actor, stage manager, deus ex machina if not Deus, and critical spectator, gives a most unusual twist to displacement and permutation.

In *Othello,* which I consider a domestic tragedy, discourse assumes many of the performative tasks that would normally devolve upon the

Moor or Iago, so much so that it can substitute for motivation in the very act of underlining character.

In *Hamlet,* the protagonist, an even more complex figure than the Duke of Vienna, shows so much reluctance in performing his assigned and indeed solemnly sworn part that his behavior resembles that of an overly sophisticated actor, reluctant to go through with his role in a trite revenge play to which he feels superior and which he does his utmost to redirect if not rewrite. And in *The Winter's Tale* performative metaphor undertakes the unprecedented task of bridging an apparently insuperable sixteen-year gap while reconciling and harmonizing several incompatible dramatic genres: tragedy, pastoral comedy, and farce.

In order to stress the theatrical side of drama, I have at times deliberately conjured away the psychological and moral meanings—the human profundity—of the six plays discussed; and the limitations of this approach will become most apparent in my treatment of the two tragedies. But as Shakespearean scholars—historical, Marxist, psychoanalytic, thematic, contextual, structural—have convincingly and successfully unearthed nearly all the profundities embedded in the plays, occasionally by quite legitimately treating characters as people, speeches as philosophy, plots as events, the time may have come for a deliberately performative but ideologically irrelevant commentary on Shakespeare as exemplary entertainer.[19] Several remarkable scholars, James L. Calderwood foremost among them, have nonetheless succeeded in treating essential dramatic and metadramatic aspects of the plays without neglecting ideological substructures, existential values, and human referentiality.[20] I have made frequent use of their discoveries in attempting to catch some of the secrets of Shakespeare's eminently theatrical practice.

TWO

Verbal Choreography
and Metaphorical Space
in *Much Ado about Nothing*

We can read a play in at least four quite different but nonetheless legitimate and overlapping ways: as a representation of reality; as a poem; as a performative score; as an actual performance. I have of course favored throughout the book the third method; but because of the prevalence of rhetoric and wordplay in a comedy where performative clues specifically and repeatedly point to music, dancing, and fashion, rather than to drama as such, poetic analysis will appear to take the place of a metadramatic if not of a performative approach during the first two sections of the chapter. Nevertheless, performative indirection in rhetoric, country dancing, counterpoint, and even in fashionable dressing leads back in the final analysis to drama, because all these socially meaningful activities result from and reveal sooner or later a theatrical basis. They do not, as in a poem, a concert, or a ballet, exist for their own sake, nor do they attract undue attention to themselves as they would in a musical comedy. In short, the place of these activities in *Much Ado about Nothing* remains functional throughout, even though many of the characters play their parts in the reciprocating manner of dancers rather than strictly as comedians. Discussion of the play will therefore focus on the verbal relationships between characterization on the one hand, and rhetoric, country dancing, and fashion on the other.

The Title

The wording of the title has attracted considerable attention, not only because it raises the expectations of the audience while refraining from stating the plot, but also because of the enigmatic presence of "nothing," a term whose very emptiness suggests various semantic possibilities, including metaphysical meanings pertaining to artistic creation.[1] To complicate matters, critics have insisted on the pun on "noting," pronounced in Shakespeare's day in the same way as "nothing;" and, to compound the puzzle, "noting" can refer both to observation, a major recurrence in a comedy rich in deception, and to musical notation, which Balthasar makes explicit in connection with his song: "Note notes, forsooth, and nothing! "(II.iii.54).[2] It would thus appear that the wording of *Much Ado about Nothing*, unlike that of *As You Like It*, does tell the audience, if only obliquely, something about the fable. Its most obvious meaning concerns genre: the expected happy ending that rewards an audience after a concatenation of threatening events has come to naught. A second and perhaps derivative meaning would consist in a witty disparagement of theater, for whatever may happen on stage has little or no impact on the outside world. Shakespeare ironically reassures his public in much the same way that Snug the joiner in *A Midsummer Night's Dream* tells the ladies in his courtly audience that they have nothing to fear from the hideous lion he impersonates. And because the expression "make an ado" glossed by Robert Sherwood in his *English and French Dictionary* (1650) as *faire des mines,* has a close rapport with acting, the first part of the title may directly involve theatricality.

Critics, however, have shown less concern for the rhetorical and prosodic suitability of the title than for its semantic range. We might define the rhetorical relationship between *Much Ado* and *about Nothing* as hyperbolic antithesis; and it so happens that this double trope programs in one way or another the entire play. Moreover, the chiasmatic structure of the title suggests cleavage, an occurrence frequently repeated throughout the comedy by means of staged as opposed to purely verbal antitheses. Hyperbole, which appears everywhere, in action no less than in language, underlines theatricality, while antithesis and chiasmus establish close connections with music and dancing by reason of their associations with counterpoint.

The cleavage in the title may owe nearly as much to phonetic as to rhetorical devices. The nasal occlusives of "much" and "nothing" frame the "as" of "ado" and "about." Moreover, the first part of the title would seem to consist of a dactyl, the second of an iamb and a trochee. Prosody—provided we relate "nothing" to musical noting—suggests dance steps, perhaps even an opening reverence. Indeed, John Davies in his *Orchestra,* a poem contemporaneous with *Much Ado about Nothing,* establishes the closest connections between poetic meter and various dances. He wittily associates measures with spondees, courantes with dactyls, lavoltas with anapests.[3] Choreographed or not, the wording of the title, compared with that of *As You Like It* or *All's Well That Ends Well,* shows far more semantic displacement and greater rhythmic complexity.

Fashions in Dancing

Several scholars have ably discussed the presence of music and dancing in the play and shown their key functions in language, plot, and characterization.[4] I propose to push their analyses, if not further, at least in a different direction by dwelling on some of the theatrical aspects of choreography. While dancing actually occurs only during the masked ball and the festivities preceding the double wedding, the characters frequently allude to dance, usually in rhetorical terms. Social dancing, from a theatrical standpoint, indirectly involves casting insofar as Don John, Borachio, and Conrade, the heavies in the show, never join the dance, while doing their utmost to mar a marriage.[5] The fact that Elizabethans identified dancing with wooing and justified it morally as a prelude to matrimony points to a certain consistency in the three villains' behavior.[6] In any event, dancing transforms wooing into spectacle and performance. Wooing, however, requires the help of rhetoric to become persuasive and lead to marriage, the traditional denouement of comedy. Not surprisingly, the author establishes at crucial moments more or less overt relationships among dance, rhetoric, and wooing, frequently by means of substitutions. No less than theater itself, each of these performative and often competitive activities abides by specific rules.

Dancing intrudes verbally on several occasions, sometimes by means of subtle allusions or even puns. In addition, activities connected in one way or another with a courtly ball—for instance, grooming and fashion, notably in hats—recur in unexpected places. Grooming pertains no less than dancing to wooing; and all three culminate in the binding festivities that end the play. Indeed, dressing appears no less performative and ceremonial than dancing itself; and both of these stylized endeavors function as metonymies of courtship. Ostentation in clothes as well as the writing of verse—the grooming, so to speak, of language—provides visible and, better still, performative signs of love. Claudio's conversion from warrior to lover strikes Benedick as a sartorial permutation: "I have known when he would have walked ten mile afoot to see a good armor; and now will he lie ten nights awake carving the fashion of a new doublet" (II.iii.14–17). His alleged insomnia does not arise from amorous expectations but from artistic ardor in creative fashion design. Actually, the kind of substitution or misplacement of energy criticized by Benedick provides just another of those graphic but reductive elements so characteristic of the play and programmed once and for all in the title. Moreover, Claudio changes because of love from physical activity to a supine position entailing still further reduction. Since in both instances he does his best to dress for the occasion, his change from warlike to courtly behavior provides just another instance of transposition. Benedick, the self-designated adversary of Cupid, disparages, according to his custom, the outward or performative manifestations of courtship rather than love itself. Borachio, the villainous enemy of Eros, in telling Conrade about his plot to ruin Claudio's love for Hero, begins with a full-fledged satire of fashion. And he wanders so far afield from his story that his friend exclaims, "But art not thou thyself giddy with the fashion too, that thou hast shifted out of thy tale into telling me of the fashion?" (III.iii.130–32). Paradoxically, Borachio has not digressed as much as Conrade suggests, for opposition to fashion goes hand in hand with vilification of and conspiracy against courtship. Although Borachio's very name stamps him as a drunkard, his accomplice may have erred in accusing

him of giddiness, an attribute that in *Much Ado about Nothing* relates essentially to the world of love and fashion while referring to
the side effects of such dizzy dances as lavoltas and cinquepaces. No
wonder Benedick can epitomize the entire play in a single statement:
"man is a giddy thing, and this is my conclusion" (V.iv.106–7). Conrade's use of "shifted" implies a misplacement or displacement analogous in some respects to giddiness. This shift, which may indeed allude to an (ex)change in dancing, takes its place among numerous
other transfers from love and courtship to their overtly performative
manifestations in costume, gesture, and word.

Beatrice, whose name promises happiness, has an even closer involvement with the dance than any other character. Dancing in the
comedy seems to originate in her, and she playfully traces back to this
activity her own origins. When Don Pedro states: "out o' question
you were born in a merry hour" (II.i.298–99), she retorts, "No, sure,
my lord, my mother cried; but then there was a star danced, and under that was I born" (II.i.300–301). She owes her birth to her suffering mother, but her merry nature, or rather her role in the comedy, to
the choreographed music of the spheres, where Davies in his *Orchestra* places the origin of dancing itself.[7] Naturally, Beatrice makes
metaphorical use of dancing far more frequently than any other
member of the cast, wittily equating the various stages of courtship
and marriage with different kinds of dancing and thereby reducing
the vagaries of the plot to the intricacies of choreography: "The fault
will be in the music, cousin, if you be not wooed in good time. If the
Prince be too important, tell him there is a measure in everything,
and so dance out the answer. For, hear me, Hero: wooing, wedding,
and repenting is as a Scotch jig, a measure, and a cinquepace: the first
suit is hot and hasty like a Scotch jig (and full as fantastical); the wedding, mannerly modest, as a measure, full of state and ancientry; and
then comes Repentance and with his bad legs falls into the cinquepace faster and faster, till he sink into his grave" (II.i.60–69).
Through the use of puns, beginning with "good time," followed by
"measure," and ending with "sink," Beatrice introduces the spatial
performance of dancing into the rhetorical fabric of the play, which
here at least reflects the inevitable giddiness of the entire procedure.
She verbally produces permutations among wooing, marriage, re-

pentance, and dance, thereby transforming means into end by the use of a reversed comparison. Previously, the irrepressible Beatrice had associated her nemesis, Benedick, or rather a composite suitor situated midway between Benedick and the melancholy Don John, with dancing: "With a good leg and a good foot, uncle, and money enough in his purse, such a man would win any woman in the world—if 'a could get her good will" (II.i.13–15). Such a person should possess, in addition to the appearance of wealth, the chief attributes of a skillful dancer in order to stand a chance as a wooer. The term "world" contains in all probability a pun on "whirled"—a pun pointedly used by Davies in his *Orchestra*.[8] Beatrice seems to suggest that the world itself must, for successful wooing, conform to a whirl—undoubtedly a feature of the Scotch jig. Benedick, the more vocal and agile half of Beatrice's compound suitor, participates in all the dances; and only in his rhyming does he fail to "woo in festival terms" (V.ii.38), while Don John's self-assertive melancholy, even without his villainy, would preclude dancing. Conrade queries, "Why are you thus out of measure sad?" (I.iii.1–2), where the expression "out of measure" hyperbolically suggests the stately dance designated by that name—a dance probably featured in the masked ball as conducive to conversation. On the whole, Beatrice's witty creation of an acceptable suitor, midway between two antithetical characters, provides just another rhetorical variation on the title. She indeed combines hyperbole and chiasmus with antithesis in order to suggest a playful albeit aporic resolution or synthesis producing a most suitable *mise en abyme* of a comedy concluded by a double reconciliation and a dance.

Proficiency in dancing usually accompanies agility in speech. Beatrice and Benedick, who never miss a ball—or a brawl—can never refrain from uttering witticisms, a propensity they will share late in the play with Ursula and Margaret, both of them habitual dancers. Feeling that Ursula talks too pointedly about Benedick and love, Beatrice asks, "What pace is this that thy tongue keeps?" only to receive the answer, "Not a false gallop" (III.iv.83–84). Both "pace" and "gallop" directly relate to dancing, for a gallop can refer to a fastpaced dance glossed as *gaillarde* in Cotgrave's French-English dictionary. Gallop, however, may also remind the audience of Beatrice's unfavorable comparisons between Benedick and a horse (I.i.61 and I.i.129). In any case, the verbal exchange between the two maidens clearly associates racy speech with dancing, both of them seen as performative.

Roles and Permutations

The reversals promised by the title reappear at crucial moments throughout the play. The so-called main plot, recounting Claudio's changing attitudes toward Hero, moves from love and praise to contempt and disparagement, then back again. Benedick and Beatrice disparage, despise and, so to speak, repeatedly make an ado of one another, only to end up in love, marriage, and grudging applause for each other's performance. Not surprisingly, the relationship between Claudio and Hero undergoes its first reversal at about the time Beatrice and Benedick, who invariably protest too much, switch from performed and perhaps self-deceiving hostility to affection.[9] The audience must wait until the final dance for both couples to reach together a state of harmony and bliss; and we can expect that the congé that must end the dance will reverse itself in marriage. Reversal, considered by Aristotle the essence of a successful tragic plot, appears in *Much Ado about Nothing* more sudden, more complete, and sharper edged than in serious drama. Beatrice and Benedick undergo their first reversal thanks to a performance ably planned and staged by Don Pedro. At the moment of reversal, the two gulls have no other recourse than to improvise new and unfamiliar parts as gracefully as possible, while experiencing difficulties in obscuring the spectacular performances on which they had built their reputation.

It would seem, however, that the prince's intervention might not have sufficed without Claudio's change, also based on a performance, this one written and staged by Borachio. As a result of this negative reversal, Claudio switches to hostility and cynicism toward women precisely when his friend begins to favor a positive attitude toward them. In a sense, they exchange roles as readily as they would dance partners; and for this reason, Claudio, instead of merely breaking with Hero, as a gentleman should, cruelly pretends to go through the marriage ceremony just to disparage and humiliate her publicly by making a spectacular ado. He behaves as though he wished to upstage Benedick by adding meanness, in both senses of the term, to the latter's hyperbolic but quite innocuous displays of misogyny.[10] Contagion, a term used by Beatrice when she questions Claudio's friendship for Benedick, may have prepared us for the former's unwonted conduct. Even the news of Hero's death as a result of his aggression produces no discernible effect on his performance despite the friar's prediction that a repentant Claudio would feel the pangs of unrequited love and remorse. We can hardly fault the friar as a psychologist, for indeed Claudio fails to conform to behavioral norms prevailing no doubt in the audience. Far from accusing the author of psychological incoherence or blindness, we should applaud him for having made the permutation complete, with hyperbole to boot! As Claudio has wholeheartedly taken over another part only to switch back just as suddenly and totally to his former position as lover, it would seem that the necessity of assuming a role outweighs any other factor, such as motivation. Claudio—no less than Beatrice and Benedick—must unstintingly alternate between antithetical castings as a devotee and a detractor of Cupid. Psychology hardly matters, for each character must enact and implement metonymically the transpositions embedded in the title. Reversals performed in this manner, unsatisfactory though they may appear from a mimetic standpoint, repeat the patterned intricacies of counterpoint and country dancing; and the characters perform as though they envisaged the festive play as a continuous and variegated masked ball. For this reason, spatial relationships prevail over motivation, while reversal functions reductively as permutation in a quasi-mathematical sense: a sudden switch in position rather than a gradual mutation from one attitude to another. This reversal of attitudes on the part of Claudio characteristically originates in the permutation contrived by Borachio: "hear me call Margaret Hero, hear Margaret term me Claudio" (II.ii.37–38).

Counterpoint and clear-cut cleavage also mark the casting of Don Pedro and Don John. For the sake of antithesis and chiasmus rather than characterization, the author has made them complete opposites—as different as "much" and "nothing." Each of the prince's qualities encounters its counterpart and reverse in his illegitimate brother. More important still, Don Pedro displays impressive dramatic skills, as befits a leader, while Don John has to pay dearly for Borachio's trite but destructive performance. Success as an entertainer definitely places the prince, together with Beatrice, Benedick, and, to a lesser degree, Hero, at the top of the hierarchy, but Don John, who has only his melancholy to display, at the very bottom.

Permutation and Rhetoric

In *Much Ado about Nothing*, it scarcely matters whether dancing originates in rhetoric, or rhetoric in dance. In any case, rhetoric throughout the comedy tends to overreach and impose itself thematically as an increase. Hyperbole, however, goes beyond mere thematics by making itself so spectacular and tangible that it fills to capacity theatrical space. The opening scene overdetermines the theme of increase, particularly in the way the full cast gradually occupies the stage. Messina not only provides the setting, but, thanks to its governor, lavishness in the form of banquets, masked balls, the hand of his daughter, and, later, that of his niece: nobody could ever accuse Leonato of holding anything back. Several scholars have seen in Messina a seat of deception and corruption, where illusion must inevitably prevail. It so happens that illusion—the very essence of theatricality—comes from the outside, from the friendly but troubling invasion of foreign warriors. Without the struggle between the prince and his evil brother, Messina would have had to remain a tranquil and, in some respects, a pastoral world, quite devoid of drama, if not of dancing.

The triumphant return of the heroes after a battle hardly more perilous than routine maneuvers suddenly transforms the carefree existence of the Messinians into playful belligerence in the guise of mostly implicit clashes between antithetical contexts, which nevertheless merge through the deft use of metaphor. Beatrice begins by transforming the absent Benedick into a non-combatant. By designating him as trencherman, carrier of contagion, and offensive ladies' man, she shocks the messenger who sees in the noble Benedick a model officer and gentleman. Her main attack consists in substituting dubious civilian activities for heroic deeds on the battlefield. As a result, the "merry war" between them quickly displaces real warfare while setting up an intricate system of substitutions and permutations that will remain dominant throughout. Paradoxically, personal relationships in peaceful Messina can assume all the violence of real skirmishes, as Benedick ruefully shows in complaining about Beatrice's cruel remarks: "She speaks poniards, and every word stabs" (II.i.222–23).

From the very beginning, even before Beatrice's disparagement of Benedick, joy itself had displayed the "badge of bitterness" (I.i.20–1), as Claudio's uncle upon hearing the news of his nephew's safe return amply shows by the shedding of tears "In great measure" (23). Joy thus personified externalizes, hyperbolizes, and reverses itself. But then, so had victory: "A victory is twice itself when the achiever brings home full numbers" (7–8). By doubling itself, victory tends through increase to negate its essence, for a battle devoid of casualties pleasantly belies our usual expectations and appears to verge on comedy.

In her first question to the messenger, Beatrice refers to Benedick as "Signior Mountanto" (I.i.27). "Montanto," an Italian word that means an upward thrust in fencing, substitutes a peacetime martial art for warfare. The addition of the letter *u* subtly suggests a fraudulent display on his part, that of a mountebank, a miles gloriosus, or both. This initial skirmish reduces Benedick's dignity even before Shakespeare affords him a chance to impress the audience by appearing on stage. In any case, the sudden change or exchange from war to peace enables such thoroughly peaceful or civilian occupations as witty conversation and courtship to display the kind of deadly combativeness they would normally replace or abolish. The ostentatious presence of warfare in purportedly peaceful endeavors and the fact that all the young males in the cast have returned in good health from a war bring to mind a figure or trope defined by French rhetoricians as *comparaison rapportée,* whereby each of the two objects compared usurps the terminology usually ascribed to the other, for instance Ronsard's upgrading of the trite comparison between a maiden and a rose by describing the former in botanical terms and the latter anthropomorphically. Double misplacements of this sort frequently recur in the course of the play. As in country dancing, where partners repeatedly become opposites but never contraries, the two poles of such double misplacements serve mainly to complement and counterpoise each other.

In disparaging her nemesis, Beatrice solidly establishes the various themes, metaphors, and tropes that through recurrence will give unity and coherence to the comedy. She decries his supposed faithlessness as slavishness to fashion: "He wears his faith but as the fashion of his hat; it ever changes with the next block" (I.i.66–67). This accusation hardly seems to fit Benedick, known mainly for his staunch opposition to courtship, but appears to program the subsequent behavior of Claudio. Actually, Beatrice's misplaced assaults preserve in the very act of missing their target the "real" and "authentic" performance of Benedick, whom she will soon marry. Her calumny, at least in the present instance, produces just another rhetorical gambit in exteriorizing a negated virtue, constancy, by its opposite, ostentatious fashion, noted for sudden and unaccountable shifts. In fashion, we encounter another programmatic indication, perfectly embodied no doubt in the spectacular costumes displayed by the cast. Fashion, as Borachio's remarks to Conrade so clearly show, hyperbolizes clothing and makes it performative. In fact, the words "much ado about nothing" provide an even more apt commentary on fashion than on the play itself. Benedick's alleged concern for sartorial display further distances him from war. It would seem, moreover, that Beatrice has anticipated on his part an inappropriate appearance at court and especially at a ball. The incorrect positioning and style of a hat in Elizabethan country dances could indeed mar the reputation of a courtier or a suitor.[11]

The irrepressible Beatrice then describes her defenseless victim as a highly contagious disease: "the Benedick" (I.i.78), diagnosed as a verbalized and verbalizing complaint, appropriate only in so far as her opponent allegedly operates in an essentially wordy universe. His name, BENEDICK—not the more usual and more passive Benedict, the English equivalent of "Benedictus," meaning blessed—would seem to derive from *bene dico*, whereby he designates himself as an eloquent speaker. Moreover, this contagion, in which we may see a pejorative avatar of the expansiveness characteristic of hyperbole and increase, provides a device for filling with words and perhaps gestures a theatrical space even before most of the performers take possession of the stage. Increase or dilation in the comedy tends to concretize itself as profusion.

In his rapid transition from war to peace, the eloquent Benedick has textuality thrust upon him. When the messenger comments, "I see, lady, the gentleman is not in your books" (I.i.67), Beatrice wittily upgrades his trite metaphor: "No. An he were, I would burn my study" (I.i.69). Her deft use of misplaced concreteness suggests spatial expansion: a study full of books, invaded by the Benedick metamorphosed into an army of words and bookworms. Verbal dilation cannot go much further or show greater activity.[12] She has transformed her adversary into an expanding script, capable of filling many a volume, and into a verbal plague, ready to infiltrate and occupy vast territories. Compared with such lexical violence, his military prowess in a tepidly contested battle dwindles into insignificance.

The triumphant entry of the "chocolate soldiers" carries in its wake a preoccupation and a theme scarcely suited to the pastoral world of Messina—money—as evidenced by the prince's greeting: "Good Signior Leonato, are you come to meet your trouble? The fashion of the world is to avoid cost, and you encounter it" (I.i.85–87). Despite his intent to flatter the governor, Don Pedro points to the inevitable drawback of generosity: expense, here designated as "trouble." He reveals, so to speak, the other side of the coin much in the same manner the messenger had dwelled on the "badge of bitterness" in the midst of joy. Because of the frequency of such alternations, we can expect that any event or statement or, for that matter, personal characteristic will tend to promote its own reversal or denial. Indeed, characterization often shuns or contradicts psychological plausibility in order to conform to the rhetorical trope and performative device of permutation. For this reason, the characters of *Much Ado about Nothing* switch without demur to whatever unlikely casting the rhetorical twists in the plot may demand of them, unlike such stars as Hamlet and Duke Vincentio, whose performative presence dominates and transcends all events and tropes. Claudio, who had accomplished "in the figure of a lamb the feats of a lion" (I.i.13–14)—whose youth belies his prowess—never succeeds in bridging the gap between warrior and suitor, unlike his stage contemporary, Shakespeare's Henry V, a heroic figure who uses dance terms in wooing Princess Kate. In order to peregrinate all the way from one role to the next, Claudio must stage within his own mind a space-filling scene:

> But now I am returned and that war-thoughts
> Have left their places vacant, in their rooms
> Come thronging soft and delicate desires,
> All prompting me how fair young Hero is,
> Saying I liked her ere I went to wars.
>
> (I.i.269–73)

His poetic speech describes the transposition within him. He personifies his thoughts, whether of love or war, and frames them within a container not unlike a stage. The term "prompting" assumes its full theatrical meaning, for not only do his desires encourage him to perform the part of lover, but they repeat the words of a half-remembered script. The orderly Claudio keeps everything in its assigned place and moment. Although he cannot conjoin the parts of warrior and suitor, he nevertheless displays the same kind of obedience to social cues in both endeavors. He loves the same way he fights—under orders—and undergoes his transposal with but little chance of increase. Naturally, this proper gentleman takes money seriously; and love opens his eyes to the pecuniary advantages of marriage with the sole heir to Leonato's estate. Paradoxically, this hero of a bloodless battle falls in love with a maiden named Hero and thus adds just another permutation in moving from war to peace or from lion back to lamb—a sheepish one to boot.

This propensity to play ostentatiously a fixed or even a stock part only to switch without warning to its opposite leads to self-designation, as though the characters felt the need to offset their precariousness within the framework of the comedy. Beatrice and Benedick conscientiously perform as enemies of Cupid and detractors of the opposite sex only to switch when their time comes to the behavior of lovers, but without conforming, in the manner of Claudio, to all the burdensome clichés attendant on such casting. Self-designation, as does everything else in the play, makes use of hyperbole in achieving (misplaced) concreteness. Benedick, who ostentatiously designates himself as a "professed tyrant" to the opposite sex (I.i.149), tries to refute the allegation that his pallor arises from unrequited love "Prove that ever I lose more blood with love than I will get again with drinking, pick out mine eyes with a ballad-maker's pen and hang me up at the door of a brothel house for the sign of blind Cupid" (I.i.222–25). He progresses from an alleged inner feeling, love, to a blatantly spectacular exteriorization: a street sign. Rhetoric itself must resort to self-designation by means of a pen—the reductive pen of popular poetry and performance—while the street sign, by flaunting mercenary sex, brings about the debasement and rejection of courtly love. Moreover, this conventional mythological emblem, tantamount to a reductio ad absurdum of love lyrics, undermines rhetoric itself. Benedick's satirical representation mirrors his ostentatious role as cynical heretic in all matters concerning love and courtship. As Benedick in this and all his other burlesque or graphic attempts at self-designation repeatedly downgrades Eros and Hymen, therefore, his sudden conversion surprises him so completely that he fails to find time for verbal adjustments; for instance, despite his cleverness and his love, he fails miserably in his attempt to write lyrical poetry, as though the satirical vein left over from his former casting still held sway over his style. For Benedick and Beatrice, self-diegesis would seem to apply to a studied performance susceptible to change through recasting. In a sense, it resembles a costume that the performer must cast off and replace on cue. Designation would for that reason have much in common with fashion: in the latter we can see a hyperbole of clothing, and in both a prevalence of ostentation.

Fashionable or not, love clothes itself in rhetoric. The prince on two occasions uses metaphors pertaining to literature in referring to Claudio's courtship: "Thou wilt be like a lover presently / And tire the hearer with a book of words" (I.i.274–75), and "Was't not to this end / That thou began'st to twist so fine a story" (278–79). The lover or, for that matter, the detractor of love must perforce gravitate toward highly rhetorical narrative. Claudio actually caps the prince's metaphors: "But lest my liking might too sudden seem, / I would have salved it with a longer treatise" (I.i.282–83). Courtship in his opinion must make itself discursive to succeed. Indeed, falling in love forces the suitor to switch from prose to verse and from ordinary attire to fashionable bravery. Thus does love lead to hyperbole and, conversely, hyperbole to love: a vicious circle or, in more modern terms, a short circuit metamorphosed by the verbal twisting of love and hyperbole into a performative spiral.

The inability to go beyond a single designation may account for Don John's dismal performative failure. In confessing to Conrade "I cannot hide what I am" (I.iii.11), he admits that he cannot step out of his stock part as melancholy villain. Although he fails to qualify as an actor, self-diegesis hardly frees him from permutation, at least in rhetoric "though I cannot be said to be a flattering honest man, it must not be denied but I am a plain-dealing villain. I am trusted with a muzzle and enfranchised with a clog; therefore I have decreed not to sing in my cage" (I.iii.27–30). Don John expresses his one-track casting in the rhetorical mode of chiasmus; and he thus repeats in his own reluctant manner the interlocking title while stating his refusal or perhaps his inability to perform. Strange as this may seem, his projected revenge, as stated by Borachio, compounds permutation, which in this instance substitutes for psychological motivation: "Proof enough to misuse the Prince, to vex Claudio, to undo Hero, and kill Leonato" (II.ii.24–25). He will even the score with his opponents in inverse ratio to his resentment against them; and the worst fate by far will befall the innocent victims who have done little or nothing to offend him. This retribution, however unsatisfactory and unsuitable it may appear, repeats once again the title while adding a perfectly counterpoised transposal typical of a country dance. Moreover, it strikes us as no less disproportionate and unaccountable in psychological terms as Claudio's switch from lover to persecutor.

The foiling of his and Borachio's plot by Dogberry and the Watch may well provide the most paradoxical reversal and transposition in the entire play. While the villains easily gull reasonably intelligent and agile people such as the prince, Claudio, and Leonato, they do not fool the asinine Dogberry and his dullards, who, by never joining the dance, belong, so to speak, in the same camp if not in the same world. In a way, they do not participate in the comedy in the same manner as the other characters but function as shallow observers, as naive spectators, as a reductio ad absurdum of the audience, in which capacity they can neither deceive nor fall prey to deception. As Borachio helpfully remarks, "What your wisdoms could not discover, these shallow fools have brought to light" (V.i.221–22). Blindness, according to Borachio's chiasmus, functions as the prerogative of an enlightened, light-footed, but uncritical elite only too eager to gull one another. This permutation between wisdom and foolishness may perhaps owe something to the beatitudes with their Christian reversals, but far more to a topos quite frequent in Shakespeare's comedies: the world turned upside down, present no doubt in Don John's inverted revenge. The Watch in overhearing Borachio's meandering narrative pushes to the point of absurdity a general tendency in the play to make visible, tangible, or concrete various abstract entities as a means of stocking performative space. Borachio in his giddy shift had personified fashion and even transformed this concept into a directing force capable of making its devotees obey its latest whim. Conrade's remark, "I see that the fashion wears out more apparel than the man" (III.iii.129–30) echoes his friend's personification while returning once again to the theme of increase or profusion, taken in a wasteful and reductive sense. No wonder Borachio's previous question: "But seest thou not what a deformed thief this fashion is?" (III.iii.115) leads the Watch to transform a figure of rhetoric into a dangerous criminal named Deformed to whom they attribute not only an identity but a history in the form of a police record. The Watch by this device people theatrical space, future as well as past, for indeed they have high hopes of apprehending the culprit.

Permutation reaches another verbal climax in Dogberry's peculiar misuse or misplacement of language. Despite his repeated malapropisms, the audience on and offstage invariably grasps his meaning, since they expect that he will persist in saying the exact opposite of what he intends. His language, which features constant transpositions where key words and their antonyms make semantic exchanges—for instance, "redemption" for "damnation," "desartless" for "deserving," "nature" for "fortune" (III.iii)—becomes performative in its own right and appears as rigorously choreographed as dance steps. From a rhetorical standpoint, Dogberry's speech abounds in chiasmus and antithesis. His verbal misplacements never

lead to negation or contradiction, no more than would a change or a
reversal of direction in a country dance.

Permutation and Theatricality

As Bertrand Evans has pointed out, most of the characters in the
play, "incurably addicted to practicing," in the sense of gulling, never
fail to succumb to the practices of others.[13] Intelligence as such can
never protect them against deception. This propensity to make fools
of others while trusting everybody's word uncritically makes them
alternate between the contradictory roles of practicer and gull, an al-
ternation that seems deliberately to defy verisimilitude. This double
propensity makes perfect theatrical sense if we perceive it in terms of
the kind of permutation that operates in country dancing. The mere
fact of engineering a practice leads automatically to a switch, where
the perpetrator becomes in turn the victim of a sting.

Much Ado about Nothing generates five fully developed plays
within the play, each of them involving practice and three of them actually staged: the prince's, Hero's, and Leonato's; two of them
mainly narrated: Borachio's and the friar's. Moreover, the two plays
so ably directed by the prince narrate several imaginary scenes recounting the passionate behavior of Beatrice and Benedick. Some
scholars have seen in Hero's production performed by an all-female
cast a mere replica of Don Pedro's all-male performance.[14] While
they do repeat one another in content, method, and goal, they differ
in at least one of the essential aspects of playwriting—style—while
reiterating, each in its own way, the rhetorical expansiveness of the
title. The switch from Pedro's prose to Hero's luxuriant lyrics may
show that the prince, who planned it all, has taken into account the
differing tastes and requirements of his two gulls. In any case, the
heightened poetic style of the second play appears to enhance and
even groom the deliberate prosiness of the first. And they relate one
to another in the typical manner of counterpoint and exchange. Both
plays make good use of rhetoric, unlike Borachio's malicious scenario, which consists in a deceptive exchange of names. While the
first play relies mainly on hyperbole to produce an effect, the second
draws its persuasiveness from a variety of tropes. Renaissance En-

gland held rhetoric and the skillful manipulation of language in high esteem and considered their effects mainly beneficial, particularly in matters pertaining to education.[15] While simple reversal might do a world of good to Benedick, Beatrice, whose "every word stabs" (II.i.223), needs in addition the sort of moral lesson that only finely attuned rhetoric can provide.

All five plays within the play occur during the interim between Claudio's proposal and the date set for the wedding, a period of elusion and suspended time during which the characters, with little help from the plot, must continually provide the audience with entertainment. As obstacles to the success of the first play, the prince sees Benedick's "quick wit and and his queasy stomach" (II.i.342), which brings up another recurrent theme, that of food, functioning here and elsewhere as a metaphor for sex and an additional instance of profusion. Don Pedro, in undertaking "one of Hercules' labors" (II.i.324–25), faces the challenge of providing palatable nourishment for a finicky brain and body, thereby associating food with rhetoric. In wondering about Claudio's newly discovered taste for orthography, Benedick too equates rhetoric with eating: "his words are a very fantastical banquet—just so many strange dishes" (II.iii.19–20). But Benedick's queasiness will unexpectedly manifest itself not in opposition to food or love but in his vehement dislike of Balthasar's singing, even though the burden of the ditty, dealing as it does with inconstancy and deception, conforms to two of his pet grievances in such matters. This inappropriate and, according to Benedick, poorly performed song should nevertheless lend itself to dancing insofar as it alludes to steps: "Men were deceivers ever, / One foot in sea, and one on shore" (II.iii.60–61). In the advice the song gives to maidens, it too repeats the title: "Converting all your sounds of woe / Into Hey nonny, nonny" (II.iii.66–67), where "all your sounds" corresponds to "much ado" and the meaningless refrain to "nothing," or as Balthasar puts it, "noting."

Hyperbole reaches a laconic climax in Leonato's comment on Beatrice's love for Benedick: "it is past the infinite of thought" (II.iii.99), which can ironically suggest unthinkable or incredible, for indeed the lady's enraged affection presently exists only in her uncle's script. Exaggeration, in thus overreaching itself, simultaneously asserts and denies an immeasurable increase. It nonetheless suits the situation, for his niece's self-deceiving railing against Benedick cries out for the strongest of countermeasures. Taken as a whole, the gulling of Beatrice, by piling one bit of "evidence" on another, closely follows the procedure of increase; and its end result consists in creating a palpably hyperbolic spectacle of Beatrice's imaginary passion. The narrative itself, as formulated by Don Pedro, Leonato, and Claudio, provides a wealth of stage directions should Beatrice ever feel the urge to enact the scenes ascribed to her.

Hero's lyrical staging, by contrasting with the prosiness of, as well as the uninspired singing in the previous play, repeats once again the chiasmus and the hyperbole suggested in the title. Indeed, the two plays combine with one another in the way feminine grace in dancing harmonizes with the bounding steps of men who in such dances as the lavolta, the gallop, and the jig tried to display their athletic abilities, often by tossing their partner into the air. Beatrice may have referred to Benedick as "Signior Mountanto" partly because of his vigorous upward thrust in Queen Elizabeth's favorite dance.

Hero begins her play with a poetic description of the scene—a scene visible to the audience but which at the Globe could hardly have rivaled the seductive charm that her words convey:

> the pleachéd bower,
> Where honeysuckles, ripened by the sun,
> Forbid the sun to enter—like favorites
> Made proud by princes, that advance their pride
> Against that power that bred it.
> (III.i.7–11)

This pathetic fallacy with its conceits and studied repetitions generates a sort of mirror image of the cast, for the restive flowers behave like willful courtiers. Hero dwells on the ideas of resilience and opposition, attitudes she expects to confront in Beatrice. The conflict between vegetation and sunlight, in suggesting a disorder in nature while merely expressing the luxuriance of the bower, compounds the falsity of Hero's precious personifications. As a result, her grooming and pruning of language appear just as inappropriate under the circumstances as Balthasar's questionable rendition of an antilove lyric.

Everything must appear contrived in both these scenes as though to hyperbolize theatrical make-believe.

Deliberate attempts at hyperbole mark the entire scene, beginning with Hero's stage directions to Margaret: "When I do name him let it be thy part / To praise him more than ever man did merit" (III.i.18–19). Hidden in the honeysuckled bower, Beatrice thus becomes the target of a double dose of exaggeration through words and setting. Hero shows her awareness of the verbal nature of this two-pronged seduction: "Of this matter / Is little Cupid's crafty arrow made, / That only wounds by hearsay" (III.i.21–23). She incorporates mythology into her staging and makes it synonymous with her own theatrical process. Her refined, verbalized, but nonetheless satirized Cupid markedly contrasts with Benedick's crude street sign. We can regard Hero's subtle Eros and Benedick's reductive travesty as hyperbole moving in opposite directions.

Hero relies once again on hyperbole in her comments on Beatrice: "But Nature never framed a woman's heart / Of prouder stuff than that of Beatrice" (III.i.49–50). Two almost antithetical types of framing appear to operate here: that of nature, functioning as an extension of the dramatist, who bears sole responsibility for casting, and that of Hero's own production, which in a sense tends to undermine the author's characterization by revising the role he had painstakingly constructed and that Beatrice had consistently performed. Hero will succeed in unframing her cousin in the very act of framing her. She indeed takes her apart by personifying her faults and making them spectacular:

> Disdain and scorn ride sparkling in her eyes,
> Misprizing what they look on; and her wit
> Values itself so highly that to her
> All matter else seems weak.
>   (III.i.51–54)

She disparages Beatrice in so adroit a fashion that the latter's beauty and brilliance stand out in sharp relief. She damns her victim with high praise; and her disparagement, at least in tone, has little in common with the cruel satire Beatrice herself had indulged in while skirmishing with Benedick. Even in her severest accusation she refrains from demeaning her cousin: "She cannot love, / Nor take no shape nor project of affection, / She is so self-endeared" (III.i.54–56). The term "self-endeared," which concludes her double-edged indictment, possesses a grace that the synonymous "self-loving" might not have conveyed. Beatrice, convicted of selfishness and self-love, must nonetheless remain thoroughly endearing.

In providing samples of Beatrice's self-endearment, Hero develops through a multiplicity of permutations the topoi of the world turned upside down and of contradiction:

> I never yet saw man,
> How wise, how noble, young, how rarely featured,
> But she would spell him backward.
> (III.i.59–61)

In order to spell her suitors against the grain, she must first of all transform them into discourse, the substance that most readily lends itself to conversion, reversal, and exchange. It would seem that Beatrice follows in her judgments of others the very same procedures that predominate throughout this comedy in which she plays perhaps the most conspicuous part.

Not only does Hero unframe her cousin, but in so doing she preempts the latter's witty role, thus displacing and replacing her as though by contamination. Her speech, while remaining undeniably poetic, becomes far more satirical than lyrical:

> If fair-faced,
> She would swear the gentleman should be her sister;
> If black, why, Nature, drawing of an antic,
> Made a foul blot; if tall, a lance ill-headed;
> If low, an agate very vilely cut;
> If speaking, why, a vane blown with all winds;
> If silent, why, a block movèd with none.
> So turns she every man the wrong side out
> And never gives to truth and virtue that
> Which simpleness and merit purchaseth.
> (III.i.61–70)

According to Hero, her cousin, repeating in this respect the entire drift of the comedy, systematically practices permutation and reduction; she willfully misreads and falsely designates men so as to assign them ridiculous roles having little relation with what wiser witnesses such as the messenger see in them. Hero may have drawn her comments from Lucretius's *De natura rerum* (IV.11.1171ff.) from the very same passage that will inspire Eliante in Molière's *Le Misanthrope*: (II.v.711–30). But the two women move in opposite directions, the first toward reductive caricature, the second toward an affirmative use of hyperbole and transposition, capable, through love, of transforming blemishes into qualities. Whatever rhetorical direction the two characters may have chosen, they have given theatricality its due by performatively upgrading their Latin intertext. Hero's play will move, however, from disparagement of Beatrice to hyperbolic and patently false praise of Benedick, who, according to Ursula, "For shape, for bearing, argument and valor, / Goes foremost in report through Italy" (III.i.96–97).

Theatrical framing can indeed go hand in hand with false or misplaced designation, notably when Claudio accuses Hero, "Would you not swear, / All you that see her, that she were a maid, / By these exterior shows?" (IV.i.36–38). The audience offstage can consider Claudio's implied designation simultaneously correct and false— false because of the girl's innocence, correct because in Shakespeare's day an actor played the part. In repudiating his fiancée, the count has recourse to preciosity, a style hardly in keeping with the situation, but ironically consonant with his former courtly manner: "But fare thee well, most foul, most fair! Farewell, / Thou pure impiety and impious purity!" (IV.i.100–101). Reminiscent of contemporaneous French preciosity—for instance, Bouchet d'Ambillou's parodic "O merveille du monde, et monde de merveille"—the count's balanced verbal permutation, which sets in motion a fugal interplay between external beauty and inner corruption, shows affinity with both counterpoint and change in dancing.[16] In his accusations, he assumes Benedick's forsaken role, "For thee I'll lock up all the gates of love" (IV.i.103), while retaining and even exaggerating his pet verbal mannerisms, as though his tongue felt duty bound to set in reverse and deny his conduct.

Theatrical framing takes a most unusual twist when self-desigation leads Leonato, perturbed by Claudio's false accusation of his daughter, to duplicate himself. The governor, who had so actively participated in the gulling of Benedick, fittingly succumbs to Borachio's scheming. His rhetorical question concerning Hero, "Could she here deny / The story that is printed in her blood?" (IV.i.119–20), takes a purely textual turn, for in his eyes the villain's concocted script has become embodied in Hero's very being. Conversely, his own ostentatious and misplaced grief leads him to reject all performances smacking of inauthenticity:

> Give not me counsel,
> Nor let no comforter delight mine ear
> But such a one whose wrongs do suit with mine.
>
> (V.i.5–7)

As counselor and consoler, only a double, only a mirror image of himself would satisfy him and, in the manner of an entertainer: "delight his ear." Moreover, this consoling clone would have to duplicate the governor's own miserable experience; he would have to

> Measure his woe the length and breadth of mine,
> And let it answer every strain for strain,
> As thus for thus, and such a grief for such,
> In every lineament, branch, shape, and form.
>
> (V.i.11–14)

Since consolation could result only from total identification between the consoler and the consoled, it would impose demands tantamount to theatrical impossibility. Leonato, in projecting himself into an unperformable part, turns into a tyrannical but frustrated spectator requiring a representation capable of coinciding point for point with his own being. All the while the audience sees in Leonato an actor mimicking an old man's baseless grief. Thus his projection of himself into an imagined alter ego devoid of any room for otherness degenerates into a representation within a performance—into the supplement of a representation. But from a theatrical standpoint, he does succeed in filling an absent stage by concretizing and dilating his supposed inner life. The governor's impossible wish reveals the limitations of theater, which at best can approximate, but never capture or possess, total identification. His aporic self-duplication generates a performative hyperbole that collapses in the very act of asserting itself—a self-denying increase.

Leonato nonetheless affirms that consolers foolishly attempt the impossible, for they

> Would give preceptial medicine to rage,
> Fetter strong madness in a silken thread,
> Charm ache with air and agony with words.
>
> (V.i.24–26)

The governor's rhetoric, by verging on the topos of contradiction, reveals still another failure of theater which, in the manner of Beatrice's name, promises to bring happiness through silken threads, air, and especially words. Unfortunately, entertainment can cheer only those who, unlike Leonato, have the power to suspend their individual cares. But the governor's hyperbole has an additional performative function, for musical terms such as "measure," "strain," "air," by accompanying and choreographing his discourse, suggest a contrapuntal movement toward and away from his stage presence.

Duplication, designation, the staging of plays within the play, characterization, peripeteia, music, poetry, and dancing repeat, each in its own way, the various rhetorical movements, in particular the permutations, programmed by the four brief words of the title. The entire comedy features a systematic increase and expansion, in space as well as time, generated by metaphor and metonomy, functioning in the manner of musical variations on a fundamental theme. *Much Ado about Nothing* has many features in common with ballet even if it does move in the opposite direction. In ballet, a limited variety of steps and gestures program a complex narrative, while in this comedy a complicated plot evokes at every turn the repetitive movements of a dance.

THREE

Music and Framing
in *Twelfth Night*

Far from leading to permutations or transpositions as in *Much Ado about Nothing,* displacements in *Twelfth Night* remain more geometrical and static. Frames, separations, and transgressions mark the relationships among the various characters as though the setting or shaping of the stage held sway over their emotions and programmed their performance. Conversely, verbal interpenetrations, notably synesthesia, seek with varied results to compensate for rigorous framing and related forms of geometrical separation or imprisonment.[1] While metaphorical framing and verbal interpenetration pervade the entire play, rhetorical tropes such as chiasmus, hyperbole, antithesis, and interchange play a subordinate part. Rhetoric for this reason has lost the power to dilate and expand that it enjoyed in *Much Ado about Nothing.* Characterization gives evidence of greater stability than in the previous play, since the dramatist has assigned a fixed role and situation to all but two members of the cast: Viola and Sebastian, both of them shipwrecked. Characterization depends less, however, on psychological continuity than on stylistic stability. The Illyrians, with varied success, try by conflicting verbal means to break out of their shell. The duke sticks to rich poetic language and listens to traditional songs, Sir Toby and his friends indulge in much more boisterous verbal and physical activities, but all along restraining frames maintain social constraints while simultaneously providing stages for the liberating Twelfth Night festivities.

Synesthesia predominates in Orsino's opening speech when he complains so bitterly, but so lyrically and so preciously, about his inability to gain access to Olivia. His poetic stance, partly by reason of its inappropriateness, bodes ill for the outcome of his quest. A gifted poet may fail in Shakespeare's plays, witness the plight of Richard II, but a skilled versifier who relies too heavily on Petrarchan conceits while making a verbal spectacle of his surfeited appetite, clearly invites defeat. And his appreciation of melancholy music—the appreciation of a consumer rather than a performer—serves essentially to elude action rather than chart its course in a manner befitting his rank. In his repeated attempts thoughout the comedy to gain a foothold by means of an enterprising messenger within Olivia's forbidden domain, he shows among other shortcomings a lack of inventiveness and performative skills, particularly when we compare him to Viola. Not surprisingly, he tries from the very beginning to overcome insuperable barriers through verbal penetration:

> If music be the food of love, play on,
> Give me excess of it, that, surfeiting,
> The appetite may sicken, and so die.
> That strain again. It had a dying fall;
> O, it came o'er my ear like the sweet sound
> That breathes upon a bank of violets,
> Stealing and giving odor.
>   (I.i.1–7)

Stephen Booth in his highly perceptive commentary on the opening passages of the play reveals the discrepancy between the audience's clear understanding of the speeches and problems arising from close analysis of their meanings: "We do not notice what Orsino says; we hear what he must be saying. We listen to nonsense as if it were sense."[2] But whatever Orsino may say or actually convey, he attempts to make up for a deficiency. Sound, taste, and smell, no doubt compensating for the Duke's deprival of the sight and touch of Olivia, appear to merge. The very notion of a surfeit transforms sound, personified by breathing, into a substance and changes Orsino into a receptacle or container, confined, as we shall soon learn, to its own frame. In short, his particular use of language, far from freeing him from love's bondage, compounds both his imprisonment and his separation. It would seem, moreover, that the duke, bereft in his amorous pursuit of two of his five senses—the two most closely involved with mastering space—must, in frustration, make the most of the remaining three, particularly in their interpenetrations which, he hopes, will help him overcome all obstacles. Synesthesia recurs in Orsino's very next speech:

> "O,when my eyes did see Olivia first,
> Methought she purged the air of pestilence."
> (I.i.20–21)

Here sight, smell, and—thanks to a pun on musical air—sound commingle. Instead of leading to heightened repetitions of a desired spectacle, his initial glimpse of Olivia serves mainly to reinforce his remaining two senses and initiate a chain of verbal interpenetrations, but without in any way reducing his spatial confinement.

Unfortunately for the duke, Olivia not only refuses to admit his messenger, but, according to Valentine, adds to spatial separation a chronological barrier:

> The element itself, till seven years' heat,
> Shall not behold her face at ample view;
> But like a cloistress she will veiled walk,
> And water once a day her chamber round
> With eye-offending brine; all this to season
> A brother's dead love, which she would keep fresh
> And lasting in her sad remembrance.
> (I.i.27–33)

By confining herself for seven long years to her chamber, she would indeed create a formidable obstacle for Orsino. Her voluntary imprisonment leads to a ritualistic performance in which, by means of veils and tears, she metamorphoses herself into the antithesis of the sun. She circles her chamber once a day casting "eye-offending brine" in lieu of rays. Food surfaces once again by means of a pun on "season."[3] "If music be the food of love," then indeed the brine of tears will enable her to preserve a dead love, implicitly compared not only to nourishment but also to a flower, perhaps a violet, requiring water and veiled sunlight. Thus the insuperable barrier separating Olivia from Orsino by no means precludes verbal analogy and permeation or prevents the merging of concreteness and abstraction. As Stephen Booth has pointed out, this narrative also has its funny side, at least if we stage in accordance with Valentine's implied stage directions Olivia's obsessive behavior; and her cloistress's ritual ironically parallels her rejected suitor's cloying lyricism.[4] Neither of them possesses the ability to transcend or sublimate their appetite for an impossible love. For the next seven years, they have reduced their performance to going around in circles within a confined space.[5] The play evidently would come to a complete stop without powerful promptings from outside Illyria—from the sea.

In the final lines of the opening scene, the duke once again puts the emphasis on misplaced concreteness while adding the merest hint of synesthesia together with a faint allusion to taste and food:

> Away before me to sweet beds of flow'rs,
> Love-thoughts lie rich when canopied with bow'rs.
>   (I.i.39–40)

Forever excluded from Olivia's enclosure, Orsino imaginatively substitutes an open chamber in a garden and thus verbally overcomes an impenetrable frame. Beds, canopied in Elizabethan times, reinforce the ambiguity between nature and a room.

More important still for my particular purpose, Orsino, in this opening scene, makes use of the key word for staging in *Twelfth Night*:

> O, she that hath a heart of that fine frame
> To pay this debt of love but to a brother.
>   (I.i.34–35)

Orsino's self-defeating praise of Olivia's otherwise merciless heart confirms in terms of money and exchange, an essential theme throughout the comedy, their utter separation. This "fine frame" happens to structure the theatrical world of love while programming all the isolating partitions featured throughout the play.

Orsino, in his early speeches, invariably maintains a high if somewhat precious poetic level without ever allowing his erotically suggestive sensuousness to degenerate into sensuality. In the scenes involving Sir Toby, Sir Andrew, and Maria, sensuality, consisting mainly in celebrating on a nightly basis the carnivalesque Twelfth Night festivities, becomes blatant, all the while perpetuating on a lower level the musical, synesthesic, and framing elements that had graced the opening scene.

Sir Toby and his companions deliberately reduce lyrical commingling to transgression and disorder. Maria stresses in her very first words Sir Toby's woeful lack of suitability: "Ay, but you must confine yourself within the modest limits of order" (I.iii.7–8). The terms "confine" and "limits" pertain to the kind of containing and constraining frame that Sir Toby at all times willfully transgresses, thus displaying a dislike for barriers no less intense, but far more explicit and effective, than that of the hemmed-in duke. He naturally objects to the hateful word "confine": "Confine? I'll confine myself no finer than I am. These clothes are good enough to drink in, and so be these boots too. An they be not, let them hang themselves in their own straps" (I.iii.9–12).[6] By his deft use of puns, the bulky knight transfers "confine" from the code of moral behavior to the more theatrical realm of clothing while describing himself, or rather his costume, as an appropriate receptacle for food and drink. He operates a farcical verbal transference, metonymic as well as metaphorical, by means of which his own transgression passes into his personified boots, threatened with hanging should they fail to comply with his wishes. The poetic exchanges between abstraction and concreteness that had marked the first scene reappear on the level of a burlesque and probably erotic parody in Maria's advice to Sir Andrew: "Now, sir, thought is free. I pray you, bring your hand to th' butt'ry-bar, and let it drink" (I.iii.63–64).[7] Music, featured in the first line of the play, frequently recurs, usually in the guise of songs and dance tunes. Sir Toby jests: "My very walk should be a jig. I would not so much as make water but in a sink-a-pace" (I.iii.116–17).

Full-fledged synesthesia, Orsino's most intricate but counterproductive verbal device, occurs in a later scene involving the two knights and Feste: "To hear by the nose, it is dulcet in contagion" (II.iii.53), a metaphor that burlesques the fusion of the senses so dominant in the opening scene, particularly in the duke's vision of

Olivia purging the air of pestilence. It would seem that language establishes a vast network capable of tying together characterization, stage sets, costumes, and story, whereby every aspect of the comedy enters into a specular relationship with all the others in spite of or perhaps because of barriers, obstacles, and separating frames. Indeed, metaphors appear no less performative than the characters themselves and characterization seems to depend on set verbal determinations programmed from the beginning, rather than on psychological verisimilitude.

Sir Toby's comic use of synesthesia, while establishing analogies with the play's lyrical overture, leads to a spectacular and noisy performance: "But shall we make the welkin dance indeed? Shall we rise the night-owl in a catch that will draw three souls out of one weaver?" (II.iii.53–56), which Malvolio in the name of his mistress will try to stop. It would seem, if we can trust Malvolio, that Olivia insists on restricting Sir Toby and his company, as well as Orsino, to their respective and respectful places. But strict obedience to her purported wishes, by curtailing Sir Toby's entertainment, might put an end to Shakespeare's own show, which, like love, can hardly survive without repeated transgressions. As theatrical displacement in this particular instance differs very little from transgression, it would follow that Malvolio's opposition to disorderly entertainment must inevitably lead to his solitary confinement, whereby he undergoes materially what Orsino and, before Viola's intervention, Olivia had suffered spiritually. Thus Sir Toby's impish attempts to cross barriers will paradoxically generate an enclosing frame far more concrete and constraining than any of the others, for he will succeed in upgrading a metaphorical construct into a performative space doubling as a stage prop: Malvolio's dark enclosure.

An even greater displacement originates on the outside. Viola and Sebastian escape from the greatest receptacle of all: the boundless main; and their shipwreck in Illyria generates sufficient power to break down all obstacles.[8] Viola, in addition, contrives a purely theatrical transference by disguising herself as Cesario, a travesty that will enable her on the level of the plot to find employment in Orsino's palace and gain access to Olivia's dwelling. She alone succeeds in combining spatial displacement, originating in her shipwreck, with a performative deviation that initially consists in stepping out of her own confining sex. The fact that only an adolescent actor could have played Viola's part in Shakespeare's day makes this redirection all the more theatrical by reason of its compounded unsuitability.

Viola/Cesario functions in the duke's household as a performing messenger forced to shuttle between the two main frames of the comedy. Orsino assigns her a task quite in keeping with her initial travesty or transgression, but unfortunately detrimental to her hidden project, by imposing upon her the tritest of scripts which he orders her to perform: "I have unclasped / To thee the book even of my secret soul" (I.iv.12–13); "It shall become thee well to act my woes" (I.iv.25). He even makes her follow precise stage directions by ordering her to transgress all barriers in a manner perhaps more suitable to Sir Toby than to her preferred type of casting: "Be clamorous and leap all civil bounds" (I.iv.20). Nevertheless, the inconsequential Orsino praises his messenger for qualities that would normally preclude such boisterous behavior but that may prepare his own eventual switch as lover from Olivia to Viola:

> Diana's lip
> Is not more smooth and rubious; thy small pipe
> Is as the maiden's organ, shrill and sound,
> And all is semblative a woman's part.
> (I.iv.30–33)

Although his stage directions seem most inappropriate, his appreciation of Cesario would appear to echo the comments of some hypothetical stage director elated at having discovered the youth most capable of assuming the part of Viola. In any case, Orsino's praise of Cesario takes us back to the origins, not of the script itself, but of its stage performance. Paradoxically, the duke cannot see through Viola's disguise even when he dwells, no doubt to the delight of the Elizabethan audience, on the perplexing displacement evidenced by this young player who shows an overwhelming predominance of pleasing feminine features, visual as well as auditory. He may have correctly assumed that, in keeping with the programming of the play, only an ambiguous and misplaced performer would possess the wherewithal to break through supposedly impenetrable but really porous barriers.

Feste the clown enjoys the same ubiquitous privileges as Viola. By staging a clever performance, he quickly succeeds in regaining a foothold in Olivia's quarters without relinquishing his position in Orsino's palace or even in Sir Toby's riotous maisonette. Unlike Viola, he has no other project or function than to entertain and no other employment than that of clown. A professional showman, he thrives on deliberate verbal and conceptual manipulations with no other aim than material gratifications tantamount to a good time for all. A pure entertainer without ulterior motives, he coincides even in name with the spirit of Shakespeare's most festive play. In Feste, the shrewd and archetypal entertainer, we witness theatrical displacement incarnate; and naturally he gains access to Olivia's presence even before Viola can deliver Orsino's message of love. Perhaps the clown's festive contagion has dissipated Olivia's spell of melancholy and broken down some of her defenses, though hardly to the advantage of Orsino. The clown's contagion may have made her vulnerable to Viola's theatrical charms, for the latter not only has disguised herself by costuming but has brought along with her a text she dutifully and pointedly performs: "I would be loath to cast away my speech; for, besides that it is excellently well penned, I have taken great pains to con it" (I.v.164–66). Viola stubbornly attempts to confine herself to an imposed text, functioning in this instance as a protective enclosure; and she refuses to answer because "that question's out of my part" (I.v.171), whereby a spatial and a theatrical metaphor join forces in expressing the messenger's complete lack of involvement in her message. She insists that the script she has had to learn by heart speaks only for Orsino. Like any normal player, she makes a sharp distinction between her identity and her casting—in this case a role some three or four times removed from her own preoccupations as impersonator and lover. To nobody's surprise, Olivia asks the messenger, who at that time cannot identify her audience, "are you a comedian?" (I.v.174).

In tête-à-tête with Cesario, Olivia queries, "Where lies your text?" (I.v.211), and when Viola answers, "In Orsino's bosom" (212), she combines in her next question spatial with textual precision: "In his

bosom? In what chapter of his bosom?" (213). Cesario playfully retorts in a way that may or may not help Orsino's suit: "To answer by
the method, in the first of his heart" (I.v.214). It remains for Olivia to
push the metaphor of textuality to its limits: "O, I have read it; it is
heresy" (I.v.215). In thus combining their talents so as to inscribe Orsino's misguided passion as just another readable and performable
script, they provide an additional example of misplaced concreteness
in which, for the first time, theatricality becomes verbally explicit,
perhaps at the expense of lyricism. Moreover, they have engineered a
transfer of emotional and spiritual values henceforth equated with
the theatrical activities of writing, memorization, and performance,
activities no less indispensable than casting to the comedy presently
unfolding.

And still further barriers collapse when Olivia, at Cesario's re-
quest, unveils: "Have you any commission from your lord to negoti-
ate with my face? You are now out of your text. But we will draw the
curtain, and show you the picture. [Unveils.] Look you, sir, such a
one I was this present. Is't not well done?" (I.v.218–22).

Carried away by her self-generated theatrical movement toward
spectacle, Olivia forgets her vow, which Valentine alone had made
known to the audience, not to show her face even to the empty sky
during a period of seven summers. Worse still, she endeavors to give a
sort of playful permanence to her transgressive display by transforming herself by dint of language and gesture into a permanent representation. She goes even further in the direction of concreteness by
making a full inventory of her face, whose features she treats like so
many negotiable items or chattels, thus expanding the mercenary
thematics of the comedy. Olivia, now framed like a portrait, exhibits
her face and, by means of an imaginary curtain, enhances her presence onstage while momentarily—and perhaps erotically—narrow-
ing theatrical space. Having deftly extirpated Viola from Orsino's
script, Olivia has the power to cut down to size—to the dimensions
of the set or portions thereof—the performative matter of the text.
She nonetheless persists in setting limits or containers even when she
eagerly consents to abolish barriers. By framing herself, and, or so
she hopes, Cesario with her, she quite reverses the direction of her
previous performance, thus transforming her own portion of the

stage into a trap and her previous invisibility into a spectacle identifiable with an artifact—with *Twelfth Night* itself. Olivia attempts to take possession of the stage, which henceforth must conform to the dimensions of her own enclosed and eroticized chamber, where she had expected to exert full control. Throughout this scene, language continuously constructs and deconstructs the stage according to the necessities of performance.[9] Through the gift of a ring and then of a miniature portrait enclosed in a jeweled frame, Olivia vicariously bursts out of her own self-imposed incarceration and attempts to bring Cesario within her orbit. For love to succeed, it must encompass the loved one with the set. The miniature as gift provides a reductive model of Olivia's role in the comedy.

While Olivia derives her performance mainly from painting and the overdetermination of a fixed frame, most of the other characters, each in a different way, favor music, closely related to porousness and penetrability. Orsino naturally expresses his passion in terms of music, preferably "antique song" (II.iv.3), connected with remembrance and thus having little chance of shaping further developments in the plot. Since he turns more to the past than to the future, his love acquires a fixity paradoxically analogous to painting:

> For such as I am, all true lovers are,
> Unstaid and skittish in all motions else,
> Save in the constant image of the creature
> That is beloved. How dost thou like this tune?
>   (II.iv.16–19)

Viola, by answering most appropriately in terms of a reverberating stasis—"It gives a very echo to the seat / Where Love is throned" (II.iv.20–21)—propels music toward three-dimensional space. Orsino's constancy functions throughout as an additional imprisoning frame—the sort of container from which Olivia, a far more effective dramatist than the duke, had so rapidly freed herself if only to impose a more dynamic and encroaching framework of her own invention. Framed in his passion and confined to the past, Orsino will require the strongest of thrusts to drag him back to the present, where he will discover the love of the free-spirited and homeless Viola.

The theatricality of framing becomes even more explicit in the main subplot, which recounts the farcical tribulations of Malvolio. On the level of the story, the undoing of Olivia's pretentious steward has little in common with the romantic loves of Orsino, Olivia, Viola, and Sebastian, even though it leads to the marriage of Sir Toby and Maria. Unlike most subplots, this one functions as a play within the play. Self-love and vanity have isolated Malvolio by relegating him to a frame of his own devising, to an inner stage where he casts himself as the star performer and from which he excludes all rivals. Other than himself and Olivia, he does not require an audience. For this reason among others, we can see in him an enemy not only of disorder and "cakes and ale" (II.iii.106), but of theater itself, which can hardly thrive in a private or restricted world. Since Maria has succeeded in inventing a plausible script coinciding with his wishful thinking, Malvolio inevitably believes that the forged letter comes from Olivia. In addition to a faintly veiled declaration of love, this epistle contains a wealth of stage directions that the steward, in costuming and gesture, will scrupulously follow. His faithful performance strikes Olivia as so preposterous that she immediately has him banished to a dark enclosure, suitable to hide mad behavior and other questionable spectacles. Maria's precise stage directions have indeed transformed Malvolio, wearing yellow stockings, cross-gartered, into a weird spectacle. A victim of textuality in his attitude and in his attire, he adds by means of a strange reversal graphics, if not a script, of his own making: "He does smile his face into more lines than is in the new map with the augmentation of the Indies" (III.ii.70–71). Sir Toby and Maria have thus caused a displacement whereby the steward externalizes and sets into a readymade frame the not-so-secret scenario of his daydreams. His virtuoso performance, in which he faultlessly interprets a script down to the least gesture, coincides with his greatest failure—a failure he enacts to the delight of the audience on and off stage. Malvolio goes so far as to utter out loud his own thoughts before, during, and after his discovery of the forged letter. Since the conspirators overhear his monologue, it would seem that Shakespeare has deliberately modified the convention requiring that only the offstage audience should hear an aside or a soliloquy. Perhaps the realization that each frame, however psychologically convincing it may appear, must inevitably turn into a public display explains this clever departure from standard theatrical practice. As thoughts throughout this comedy tend to materialize into spectacle, we may also ascribe the steward's propensity to think out loud to the metaphorical programming of the play.

Spectacle of an analogous nature characterizes the farcical duel between Cesario and Sir Andrew, both of them considered suitors to Olivia's hand. Sir Toby tells his gull, "you are now sailed into the North of my lady's opinion, where you will hang like an icicle on a Dutchman's beard, unless you do redeem it by some laudable attempt either of valor or policy" (III.ii.23–27). Sir Toby's comic metaphors relate the subplot not only to Viola's shipwreck but also to Malvolio's newly charted grin. Sir Toby's literary theories lead to the transformation of Sir Andrew's challenge to Cesario into a script: "Go, write it in a martial hand. Be curst and brief; it is no matter how witty, so it be eloquent and full of invention. Taunt him with the license of ink. If thou thou'st him some thrice, it shall not be amiss; and as many lies as will lie in thy sheet of paper, although the sheet were big enough for the bed of Ware in England, set 'em down. Go about it. Let there be gall enough in thy ink, though thy write with a goose-pen, no matter. About it!" (III.ii.37–44). Sir Toby provides an abundance of directions for this performative text, rich in gestures as well as words and appropriately set in an expandable frame: a sheet of paper capable, if necessary, of obliterating a large section of the stage. Sir Andrew's challenge should in addition produce synesthesia, for the trite "gall in ink" metaphor happens to combine taste with color. Actually, the rotund knight attempts to stage an impossibility: "I think oxen and wainropes cannot hale them [Sir Andrew and Cesario] together" (III.ii.53–54). He thus expects to drag each one metaphorically out of his habitual frame, identical in this instance with a cowardly or effeminate role. Sir Toby, one of several surrogate dramatists in the play, succeeds in transforming his victims into reluctant puppets, and he forces them to display their inadequacies in the form of pure spectacle.[10]

The no less spectacular confusions between Viola and Sebastian depend for their staging on another theatrical convention, for the former never manages to hide her femininity, while the latter invariably performs in a manly fashion. It would seem, therefore, that their shipwreck has only partially freed them, for they always return to their original casting. The unlikely confusions of the other characters not only lead to comic situations, but manifest, as spectacle and performance, the porousness characterizing language throughout the play and thus mirror in a peculiar fashion the verbal interpenetrations and synesthesic mixtures so prominently featured in *Twelfth Night*'s poetic overture.

The overdetermination of porousness and framing in the comedy may compensate for the inevitable shortcomings, noted elsewhere by Shakespeare himself, in the props and scenery of Elizabethan staging.[11] By materializing through metaphor those spectacular features that a director for want of technical means cannot display to an expectant audience, language constantly comes to the rescue of visible staging. Since space through a multiplicity of variegated theatrical frames tends to predominate, time in spite of its close connection with music has a somewhat subordinate but nonetheless essential function. It takes Viola's "most happy wrack" (V.i.258) to set time in motion. Without the shipwreck, Olivia might have wasted seven uneventful years circling her tear-stained chamber while forcing Orsino to console himself with musical and poetic surfeits far less substantial than Sir Toby's.

Time throughout the play tends to make its presence theatrically tangible as haste. Olivia after her escape from a constraining frame never wastes a moment and even marries Sebastian in a rush. Similar haste marks the invention, performance, and outcome of the plot against Malvolio. Action appears to speed up as the comedy unfolds; and progressive acceleration makes the various frames spin toward one another until they all come together at the denouement. Generosity and lavishness, in keeping with the title, increase as time reaches its greatest celerity and as the frames finally telescope. And this increase not only surfeits the performers' and the audience's appetite but results in a ritualistic plenitude suitable to the festivities and even the etymology of the Epiphany.[12] As Stephen Booth has stated, "audiences of *Twelfth Night* feel good," but hardly because of the joyous and liberating quality of the play, for "much of our joy in *Twelfth Night* derives from triumphant mental experiences like our modest but godlike achievement in comprehending scene 1," where the audience makes sense of nonsense. I submit that the triumphant mental experience of the spectators includes not only an understanding of the speeches, but a perception of the performative constraints imposed upon the characters.[13] The performative actions of comedy induce performative reactions on the part of the audience.

FOUR

Performative Staging
in *Measure for Measure*

As we might expect in a play dominated by a single character and frequently deriving mundane metaphors from sacred texts, notably from the parables, metatheater and intertextuality stand out far more clearly than in *Much Ado About Nothing* and *Twelfth Night*. While framing functions overtly and even explicitly for the purpose of continually resetting the stage, it no longer pervades the language of the comedy to the same extent as in *Twelfth Night*. Permutation once again becomes a dominant factor, but never to the point of replacing or seriously undermining motivation. After all, Shakespeare has not provided interludes for dancing and playing music in this dark comedy, where elusion must forsake its previous connections with entertainment. Permutation in *Measure for Measure* arises from metaphorical structures—for instance, from the often paradoxical relationship between death and sex, or more subtly from allusions to the beatitudes and their promise of reversals.

The comedy begins with a false exit enabling the protagonist to move at will to and from the center of the stage. Nothing whatever comes from outside Vienna, and Duke Vincentio actually has to direct and perform his return to a position and place he had never relinquished. This initial transfer sets in motion and, in a sense, programs all subsequent peripeteia, much in the same manner that the title in *Much Ado about Nothing* and the initial framing in *Twelfth Night* metonymically determine the unfolding of the plot and the modalities of characterization. From a metadramatic standpoint, Angelo functions as a dubious understudy for the duke, who casts himself in the part of a friar. But Vincentio's deputy does not really enjoy the usual prerogatives of a ruler, though hardly because his master has imposed limitations on his power or delegated solely the authority to punish sexual transgression. But it so happens that the only dangerous criminal and potential enemy of the state mentioned in the play, the notorious pirate Ragozine, conveniently succumbs to a fever without ever needing to display his fearsome presence on stage. It would appear, therefore, that Angelo must perforce reduce the scope of his office to a single executive capacity. The duke, moreover, has chosen his replacement with the stated expectation that the latter would reactivate a law fallen into disuse and play a part far different from, and even antithetical to, his own—indeed, a part that Angelo has never stopped performing: that of doctrinal rigorist, a role not exactly suited to a humanist who excels at playing God, both Christian and ex machina.

Critics from John A. Heraud back in 1865 to Louise Schreiner have wondered at the biblical intertextuality of the comedy.[1] *Measure for Measure,* which starts with the parable of the talents, ends with that of the wise and foolish virgins. Many subtle and inspired scholars, including G. Wilson Knight, have ably assessed the duke's degree of holiness or perversity thoughout the play.[2] I do not intend to question or justify the duke's or any other character's motives or morality but merely to discuss their theatrical appropriateness at the risk of neglecting the undeniable intellectual profundity of this problematic masterpiece. In any event, Vincentio pretends to entrust Angelo with the leading role but without deigning to supply a script. The substitute has thus received full license to improvise his own scenario, whose unfolding the duke will observe, so to speak, from a hidden lóge.

Far from delegating his powers to a truly creative dramatist, Vincentio has passed them on to a reductive character obsessed with legal and sacred texts dictated countless years before the opening of the play and invariably condemning illicit sex. This delegation or transfer of power actually undergoes metonymic twists; the duke tells Angelo, "be thou at full ourself" (I.i.43), adding, "Mortality and mercy in Vienna / Live in thy tongue and heart" (I.i.44–5). Metonymy involves in this instance political potency, for Angelo has received from his sovereign not only the power of life and death but also a theatrical function; and in order to follow literally the instruction "be thou at full ourself," he would literally have to impersonate his master. Angelo's response adds still another metonymy, a trope well suited for orderly theatrical unfolding and frequently used in this play:[3]

> Let there be some more test made of my mettle
> Before so noble and so great a figure
> Be stamped upon it.
>   (I.i.48–50).

Worthy or unworthy, the deputy transforms himself into the talent of the parable. The remainder of the play will test and assay his "mettle," which, do what he will, must inevitably fail to represent the likeness of the duke. Angelo ironically does himself a disservice, for his metaphor unwittingly brings out the mercenary attitudes that, as we shall soon learn, have heretofore marked his behavior and which will prevail in the near future. Money (in which we may see a reductive misplacement of the parable of the talents) and exchange play a no less important part than the biblical intertexts and usually tend to put into question a character's moral values and motivation.

Some four years before his election, Angelo had broken his promise to marry Mariana because she had lost her dowry, and adding insult to injury, he had maliciously slandered her. In the course of the play, he will contract to buy Isabella's favors and then refuse to pay his debt. In a sense, Angelo, despite or by reason of his proclaimed rigorism, stands in the same relationship to love as do Mistress Overdone, the clown Pompey, and their slanderous client Lucio, most fittingly condemned at the end to marry the whore he had previously mistreated.[4] Angelo's broken promises point to an unwillingness or perhaps even an incapacity on his part to bring to a conclusion the various scenarios he has set in motion. As dramatist, he makes the mistake of abandoning plots in mid-course. Furthermore, his brief and oblique acceptance speech brings up the issue of representation, implicit in all theater: to what extent does he possess the capacity to represent and play the part of Vincentio—to perform, so to speak, as his stand-in, in both senses of the term? The substitution of Angelo will indeed entail a loss, a descent, a displacement to a lower level, performative and otherwise. Far from doing Angelo a favor, the duke, theatrically speaking, has placed him in a double bind whereby the deputy runs the risk of immediately having to assume a new and unrehearsed role while vainly trying to perpetuate the studied part on which he had built his reputation. His new casting inevitably removes him from his usual dismal employment without providing any of the promptings he would need in order to fit into a part demanding the inventiveness of a skilled dramatist. He indeed will fail in the latter capacity and will soon compose a villainous drama which, he devoutly hopes, will never receive a public audition. And this new play merely repeats, with compounded treachery, his previous breach of promise. He remains all along a prisoner of his own intertexts, originating in the Old Testament, while entrapping himself in those of the duke and Isabella, derived mainly from the Gospels.[5] His repudiation of an innocent and loving fiancée shows at the very least his lack of affinity with the bridegroom in the parable of the wise and foolish virgins.

In his own displacement from stage to stage, His Grace Duke Vincentio preserves his theatrical integrity while improvising a new part and assuming a new dramatic function. By burdening Angelo with the semblance of temporal power, the duke facilitates the enactment of spiritual potency that, as ruler, he also represents. Upon his false departure, he shows distaste for the usual rewards of good theatrical or political performance: "loud applause and aves vehement" (I.i.70), which in this instance would hinder his passage from the limelight of power to the equally spectacular and, as Rosalind Miles has stated, conspicuous post of vigilant observer.[6] Although he asserts, "I love the people, / But do not like to stage me to their eyes" (I.i.67–68), Vincentio nevertheless reserves the right to perform quite differently during his staged return. Displacement can relate no less to space than to hierarchy—sometimes simultaneously to both of them, including the position occupied by a performer on the stage.

Similar exchanges operate at every level, including of course the lowest, if only for the sake of dramatic emphasis. In telling Mistress

Overdone, "Though you change your place, you need not change your trade" (I.ii. 104–5), Pompey reveals that although Angelo has literally forced the removal of every bawd and house of ill repute in or near the city, he has not for all his efforts put an end to mercenary love, including above all his own. With constable Elbow, displacement becomes synonymous with verbal misplacement, echoed in the final act by Lucio when he attributes his own slanderous remarks to the duke disguised as a friar. The same Lucio at his first appearance onstage had playfully given language a helping hand in relating and even collapsing spiritual and mundane meanings: "Grace is grace, despite of all controversy: as, for example, thou thyself art a wicked villain, despite of all grace" (I.ii.24–26). Lucio, who has the ability or rather the audacity to penetrate everywhere, functions with equal aplomb and unsuitability at all levels. A faithful customer of Mistress Overdone, a bosom companion of Claudio, he ranks a fairly close second to his antithesis, Duke Vincentio, as a perpetrator of substitutions. In serving as Claudio's messenger to Isabella, he scales the dizzy heights that separate the debased world of Pompey from the spirituality of a Clarist convent. Shakespeare refrained from choosing a more decorous go-between such as Friar Peter, for he may very well have needed the conjunction of corruption and saintliness to induce a further dramatic change in Angelo. Isabella certainly possesses all the attractions capable of setting the deputy in motion. As her brother claims, "in her youth / There is a prone and speechless dialect, / Such as move men" (I.ii.177–79). In addition to such nonverbal attainments, "she hath prosperous art / When she will play with reason and discourse, / And well she can persuade" (I.ii.179–81). In her confrontation with the deputy, her physical assets will naturally prevail over her rhetorical gifts; and her eloquence will serve only to aid and abet sex appeal. Angelo, who "scarce confesses / That his blood flows" (I.iii.51–52), and Isabella, who aims at imposing upon her convent "a more strict restraint" (I.iv.4), have a common origin and, at the inception of their encounter, share a common intransigence. The former has just begun his journey toward temporal power, however, while the latter has had to postpone her final retreat to unworldliness. By interceding for her brother, she interrupts and suspends her intended casting in a definitive role. In this respect, it would seem that the drunken Barnardine, who has retreated to a permanent state of unfeeling degradation, serves no other purpose in the comedy than to function as her antithesis.[7]

Isabella's opening disclaimer does little to further her brother's cause:

> There is a vice that most I do abhor,
> And most desire should meet the blow of justice,
> For which I would not plead, but that I must,
> For which I must not plead, but that I am
> At war 'twixt will and will not.
>
> (II.ii.29–33)

Like Angelo and even Vincentio, she inevitably gets caught up within the limits set by the play, whereby power restricts itself to the administration of justice and sexual transgression becomes, so to speak, the only felony. In beginning her plea, she puts herself squarely on the side of Angelo, for she fails to justify her intervention in her own eyes and attempts to elude the part her sisterly duty should impose upon her. Nor would it appear that she pretends to agree with the deputy merely to win him over. She most certainly needs the encouragement of Lucio, who, far more than her condemned brother, belongs, as a habitué of Mistress Overdone, in the opposite camp. Lucio directs her, prompts her, coaches her, behaves at first like a disapproving audience, and ends up by enthusiastically applauding her performance. Her pleading appears all the more theatrical because her words, by militating against her convictions, produce a cleavage within her. Her spectacular role as intercessor sharply conflicts with her subdued part as novice, which at the beginning of her confrontation with Angelo she insists on perpetuating. Thanks to her prompter, she willy-nilly progresses toward sexuality, a transformation that will gradually move if not improve the heretofore frozen Angelo. The provost's aside at the beginning of her plea: "Heaven give thee moving graces!" (II.ii.36), contains a double ambiguity, for "moving" can designate love as well as pity, while "graces" can refer equally to divine influence and to feminine charms, thus adding a further quibble to Lucio's initial play on the word "grace." The Provost's wish will come true, but only because the secular sense of his words has more than enough power to prevail. Indeed, secularization always has the last word in this play, dominated by religious allusions.

Lucio's able stage directions work like magic. He coaches the novice as he would a gifted but still inexperienced performer, slow to warm up to a new part: "Kneel down before him, hang upon his gown; / You are too cold" (II.ii.44–45). In kneeling, she assumes the posture of suppliant, a carryover from her religious practices; but at the same time, by following Lucio's directions, she, in all innocence, thrusts her seductive gracefulness on Angelo. Her argument and her style become progressively more persuasive and poetic the more she moves away from her initial casting and into the role presently forced upon her, which she had deliberately tried to elude. Paradoxically, the prompting of Lucio leads her to plead against herself and perform bodily gestures capable of making Angelo's frozen blood flow only too hotly. Her first really convincing arguments make full use of a theatrical code:

> Well believe this,
> No ceremony that to great ones 'longs,
> Not the king's crown, nor the deputed sword,
> The marshal's truncheon, nor the judge's robe,
> Become them with one half so good a grace
> As mercy does.
> (II.ii.58–63)

The "crown," "sword," "truncheon," "robe," each one a representation of office, can function as costume or prop while providing metonymies of power. And because grace once again combines gracefulness with religion, symbol moves toward a staged spectacle.[8]

In pursuing her plea, the novice has recourse to a transposition of identities or, in theatrical terms, of roles:

> If he [Claudio] had been as you, and you as he,
> You would have slipped like him; but he, like you,
> Would not have been so stern.
> (II.ii.64–66)

This purely hypothetical displacement and chiastic exchange—an avatar of the play's title—echoes the switch from one role to another taking place within her and, presumably, within Angelo.

Isabella then goes a step further by involving her own identity:

> I would to heaven I had your potency,
> And you were Isabel; should it then be thus?
> No, I would tell what 'twere to be a judge,
> And what a prisoner.
>   (II.ii.66–69)

She hypothetically changes places with the deputy, just as later in the comedy she will physically change places with Mariana. This imaginary exchange or substitution may go further than superficially similar reversals in *Much Ado about Nothing,* for it combines performative exchange with a conceptual gap—the rift between potency and imprisonment. Thanks to Isabella's wishful permutation or reversal, we see place and power clearly arrayed against deprivation.

The novice, by means of a rhetorical question, invokes still another kind of cleavage and exchange, this time involving heaven: "How would you be, / If He, which is the top of judgment, should / But judge you as you are?" (II.ii.75–77). Her words succeed in maintaining precisely the same disproportion as before—the gap between an all-powerful judge and a "forfeit of the law" (II.ii.71). Angelo, upstaged by the novice's eloquence, moves away from his role of responsible judge and, instead of acting in his own name, substitutes an abstraction: "It is the law, not I, condemn your brother" (II.ii.80). This prudent retreat coincides no doubt with his own incipient conversion from frigidity to warmth—and thus to a newly imposed role, or rather to a compelling part he had so far repressed and whose sudden emergence catches him completely by surprise. And this substitution inevitably leads him to personify the law—to transform it into a character: "The law hath not been dead, though it hath slept" (II.ii.90). By abandoning his role as supreme judge and by transforming the law into a conscious being who sleeps, wakes, sees, decides, and enforces, Angelo attempts to elude the trap of Isabella's substitutions, only to leave himself open to temptation.

Cornered once again by Isabella, Angelo can find a makeshift defense only in a hurried transposition of meanings, though not in so radical a manner as Constable Elbow in his frequent verbal permuta-

tions, where he says the opposite of what he means, confusing among
other things "benefactors" with "malefactors," "detest" with "protest." When the novice begs Angelo to show some pity (II.ii.99), he
not too subtly changes the meaning of the word, somewhat after the
fashion of Lucio's quibbling with grace:

> I show it most of all when I show justice,
> For then I pity those I do not know,
> Which a dismissed offense would after gall,
> And do him right that, answering one foul wrong,
> Lives not to act another.
>   (II.ii.100–104)

The unknown subjects to whom he would refuse this novel kind of
pity would, at worst, resent a permissive attitude reminiscent of Vincentio's; and the hypothetical repetition of "one foul wrong" would
hardly endanger the population of Vienna except perhaps by increase. Angelo's verbal twistings force Isabella to fly from supplica-
tion and persuasion into an aggressively passionate speech, rich in
theatrical metaphors and opening the way for gestures capable of enhancing her physical charms:

>   man, proud man;
> Dressed in a little brief authority,
> Most ignorant of what he's most assured—
> His glassy essence—like an angry ape
> Plays such fantastic tricks before high heaven
> As makes the angels weep; who, with our spleens,
> Would all themselves laugh mortal.
>   (II.ii.117–23)

The word "dressed," in ironically reducing authority to costume,
stresses once again the idea of stage performance. Authority—in this instance Angelo's, since the opening scene "dressed with the duke's
love"—provides a farcical spectacle in which the disproportion between man and "high heaven" fully measures the displacement. The angels, whom one would normally expect to weep at the sight of man's,
and specifically Angelo's, shabby tricks, thanks to the adjunction of
spleens, freely join Shakespeare's worldly audience in laughter. But

these angels, unlike most of the paying spectators, might also sorrow at the spectacle of a newborn whoremaster prompting a saintly nun.

Isabella not only questions Angelo's authority but boldly supplies him with stage directions for a closet performance:

> go to your bosom,
> Knock there, and ask your heart what it doth know
> That's like my brother's fault; if it confess
> A natural guiltiness such as his is,
> Let it not sound a thought upon your tongue
> Against my brother's life.
>   (II.ii.136–41)

This time Isabella describes displacement as a large gulf fixed within Angelo, whereby his own self, transformed into a player, separates from his bosom now changed into a metaphorical stage in which his heart has elected residence. In addition, Isabella alludes to Christ's similar question to the self-righteous crowd intent on lapidating an adulterous woman. In any event, the novice transforms her adversary into a stage where two aspects of his casting come into conflict in the same manner as rival performers in a play. His aside, "She speaks, and 'tis / Such sense that my sense breeds with it" (II.ii.141–42), ambiguously combines, as William Empson has shown, intellectuality with sensuality, revealing that Isabella has moved him by her performance, which consists in transforming spirituality into representation, where it cannot help but lose its innocence.[9] Her suggestive bribery of Angelo, not by gold but by prayers, produces a powerful effect on him, for in an aside he admits his temptation in terms of a doubly displaced or displacing motion: "Amen! For I / Am that way going to temptation, / Where prayers cross" (II.ii.157–59). Unlike other sinners in the comedy, Angelo sees evil in terms of an insuperable gap: "Dost thou desire her foully for those things / That make her good?" (II.ii.173–74). He concludes: "most dangerous / Is that temptation that doth goad us on / To sin in loving virtue" (II.ii.181–83). Temptation appears to lie in the cleavage itself, a rift that paradoxically leads to permutation. The presence of the kneeling Isabella, prompted by Lucio, has vastly increased the initial change brought about by Angelo's sudden move or advancement from one role to another.[10] The gap within him, precipitated by his unexpected casting as head of state, explains why he so readily makes himself guilty of far greater transgressions than any other character, of felonies related in one way or another to the biblical intertexts that may have generated him, notably the story of David's plot against Uriah. Obviously, cleavages of this sort do not obsess Claudio, whose indiscretion, originating in his preference for property over propriety, takes on the semblance of a purely profane text: "The stealth of our most mutual entertainment / With character too gross is writ on Juliet" (I.ii.149–50). Possessed with such a script, does Juliet still require a written contract?

In falling into temptation, in trying to conceal his crime, and unlike Mistress Overdone's honest patrons, in refusing to pay for services rendered, the deputy dissociates his identity or, in terms of the play, his casting from the roles imposed upon him both by himself and by his master. As he has no other means of escape than the eminently theatrical device of keeping up false appearances, he reduces his public activities to an empty performance and his private action to illicit sex: "Heaven hath my empty words, / Whilst my invention, hearing not my tongue, / Anchors on Isabel" (II.iv.2–4). The relationship, or rather the lack of one, between his words (consider the metonymic tongue) and his imagination (invention suggests the creative activities of a dramatist) entails personification. In any case, the anchoring of his invention indicates spatial stability in one part of himself, vain motion in the rest. This discrepancy will soon result in a dissociation between conception and textuality:

> heaven in my mouth,
> As if I did but only chew his name,
> And in my heart the strong and swelling evil
> Of my conception. The state, whereon I studied,
> Is like a good thing, being often read,
> Grown sere and tedious; yea, my gravity,
> Wherein, let no man hear me, I take pride,
> Could I, with boot, change for an idle plume
> Which the air beats for vain.
>   (II.iv.4–12)

Angelo succeeds in concretizing words by the metaphor of chewing and in materializing thought through his use of the adjectives "strong" and "swelling." By this device, the frequently referred to metaphorical space within him acquires a sort of expanding solidity, akin in some respects to the numerous staging spaces that reappear throughout the comedy.

This external theatrical displacement, allowing the audience to move from a prison cell to the gates of Vienna, from a Clarist convent to a bawdy street scene, results from, corresponds to, or leads toward internal and verbal upheaval. Even gravity, the term most appropriate to Angelo's forsaken role as rigorist, remembers, by this recurrent movement toward concretion, its etymology. His gravity thus materialized and transformed into spectacle changes into a role reminiscent of that of a costumed courtier. Not surprisingly, Angelo develops the topos of theatricality, first in spatial, then in textual metaphors:

> O place, O form,
> How often dost thou with thy case, thy habit,
> Wrench awe from fools, and tie the wiser souls
> To thy false seeming! Blood, thou art blood;
> Let's write "good angel" on the devil's horn,
> 'Tis not the devil's crest.
>   (II.iv.12–17)

Temptation has by now completed the already miscast deputy's metamorphosis into a hopelessly confused actor. He has to combine antithetical parts: that of authority, wherein he has betrayed the Duke, and that of gravity, which he no longer possesses. He now sees both authority and gravity as illusory; and his decision to play the part of hypocrite so as to hide the discrepancy between acceptable appearance and the abeyance within him, where he conceals his newly acquired role of lecher, leads to another text, that of "good angel," his own name, former identity, and present appearance scripted on the devil's horn.[11]

In his second confrontation with Isabella, he reiterates the metaphor of coinage he had used in all modesty when Vincentio had appointed him his deputy:

Ha! fie, these filthy vices! It were as good
To pardon him that hath from nature stol'n
A man already made, as to remit
Their saucy sweetness that do coin heaven's image
In stamps that are forbid.
                    (II.iv.42–46)

In order to equate murder with illegitimate birth, he combines the coining of counterfeit money with the biblical statement that God created man in his own image. This metaphoric medley, heightened by an oxymoron, brings out once again Angelo's mercenary bent, alludes to the parable of the talents, reminds the audience of his own base "mettle," and prepares the illicit exchange that he will soon force upon Isabella. Throughout this scene, he brings love down to the depths of prostitution. Amongst a concatenation of terms designating money and commerce—"account," "credit," "treasures," "cheaper," "redeeming," "redemption," "ransom," "profiting," the idea of redemption stands out because of its religious implications. Isabella asserts: "lawful mercy / Is nothing kin to foul redemption" (II.iv.112–13), where "foul redemption" can readily pass for an oxymoron, a trope highly characteristic of a play that equates death with fornication and that indeed stages a gigantic permutation between living and dying.

The duke, who had initiated substitution on a political level, remains from beginning to end the chief displacer and redeemer. No less eloquent than Isabella, he knows how to manipulate meanings for every occasion. In playing the part of friar, he relishes the related topoi of contradiction and of the world turned upside down, both of which he puts to edifying use in consoling the condemned Claudio. In his highly poetic inventory of well-known religious paradoxes concerning mortality, death remains steadfast while life evinces a double movement toward and away from its other as though to echo the fugal interplay of elusion and illusion characteristic of theater: "Merely, thou art death's fool, / For him thou labor'st by thy flight to shun, / And yet run'st toward him still" (III.i.11–13). Like theatricality itself, the more life, personified and thus transformed into a character in the play, tries to elude the inevitable, the more it becomes the pawn of illusion and hurries on toward its final negation. The duke, in his own peculiar way, deconstructs life or rather its alleged process: "Thou art not thyself, / For thou exists on many a thousand grains / That issue out of dust" (III.i.19–21). By means of this systematic recourse to personification, the natural cycle undergoes a metamorphosis tantamount to the theatrical reversal of origins, manifest in the permutations happening all along on the level of the plot and within most of the characters, including the speaker himself. It remains for Claudio to epitomize the paradoxes and contradictions featured in the sermon: "To sue to live, / I find I seek to die, / And, seeking death, find life" (III.i.42–43). Claudio, however, merely verbalizes, in the tone of resignation, the very act for which Angelo has condemned him to die. The Elizabethan cliché equating love with death gives a secular twist to Vincentio's consolations. Power in Vienna, as I have already suggested, confines itself to the administration of justice; and justice limits itself to the punishment by death of male sex offenders. In other words, life-giving love becomes synonymous with dying; and Pompey the bawd can double as the acolyte of Abhorson, the executioner with a telltale name.

It would seem that Shakespeare has created a gigantic tautology wherein the entire displacement and permutation between life and death ends up as no more than a verbal difference and a trace. This clandestine equation may explain why the duke imposes marriage on his guilty deputy instead of enforcing the fatal verdict that some righteous critics would have preferred. Thus the erotic transposition between life and death, in reiterating Vincentio's false departure from Vienna, mirrors the make-believe, self-asserting but also self-negating, world of the stage. The duke's subsequent substitution of the head of a criminal for that of Claudio and the replacement of Isabella by Mariana merely develop the initial metonymy. The hopelessly misplaced Angelo must inevitably fall for these tricks, the first of which requires the expertise of a makeup artist.

Claudio, in confronting his sister, dwells on the love-death relationship: "If I must die, / I will encounter darkness as a bride, / And hug it in mine arms" (III.i.83–85). Isabella naively finds Claudio's poetic personification reassuring, even though his choice of words puts him only too solidly on the side of life at its erotic height. His inevitable reversal naturally catches the innocent novice by surprise. Unthinkable death, dissociated from sex, strikes poor Claudio as hideously repulsive: "To lie in cold obstruction, and to rot, / This sensible warm motion to become / A kneaded clod" (III.i.119–21). The love-death metaphor breaks down, at least for the moment, since "warm motion" can in no way relate to "cold obstruction," even though Angelo has done his utmost to combine the two. Isabella's revulsion at her brother's reversal has comic overtones:

> O fie, fie, fie!
> Thy sin's not accidental, but a trade;
> Mercy to thee would prove itself a bawd,
> 'Tis best that thou diest quickly.
>   (III.i.148–51)

Not only must her brother die, this time without benefit of fornication, but he must aporically descend to the basest form of sex. By the most unrewarding of exchanges, Mercy, so far identified with spirituality, becomes a bawd by means of an antithetical switch and thus undergoes a secularizing metamorphosis similar to that of redemption and no less disquieting.

The duke, who all along functions as main dramatist, chief director, master of puppetry, and privileged spectator nevertheless shows a morbid fear of displacement. What he readily does unto others, he does not suffer others, at least those of lower rank, to do unto him. This elusion may explain at least in part his dislike of, and the ignominious marriage he inflicts on, the lapwing Lucio, who had merely committed the unforgivable theatrical sins of questioning the duke's role and, worse still, of repeatedly interrupting his performance. In a brief soliloquy, Vincentio emphasizes the idea of place, taken in the senses of rank, position, and spectacle: "O place and greatness, millions of false eyes / Are stuck upon thee" (IV.i.59–60). High position transforms its possessor into a spectacle eminently vulnerable to the false perceptions, distortions, and lack of judgment of the public. True merit becomes illusory because lowly subjects, political groundlings, function as so many amateur dramatists eager to foist on any audience their mediocre scenarios. Not surprisingly, these multifarious spectacles generate and give way to scripts:

O place and greatness, millions of false eyes
Are stuck upon thee; volumes of report
Run with these false, and most contrarious quest
Upon thy doings; thousand escapes of wit
Make thee the father of their idle dream,
And rack thee in their fancies.
　　　　　　　　(IV.i.59–64)

Vincentio, who even more than other Shakespearean rulers combines the functions of audience, dramatist, and stage director, now
sees himself as the target of his subjects' competing inventions as well
as the misplaced origin of their idle efforts at dramatic creation. The
duke, by favoring the topos of a topsy-turvy world, had actually invited the reversal of his own prerogatives.[12] Moreover, as a character
in a play, he points to all the interpretations and misinterpretations,
including of course my own, to which spectators, readers, and exegetes have forever subjected him. Hamlet, Vincentio's nearest contemporary in point of composition, will maliciously trick not only
King Claudius and his court, but succeeding generations of critics
down to this very day.

The general movement toward spectacle and performance becomes more explicit soon after the duke undergoes and presumably
recovers from his crisis in representation: it reaches a climax as the
comedy draws to a close. Staging becomes all important; and indeed
the duke gives express orders concerning the solemn ritual of his
mock return, in the course of which he performs in the manner of a
skilled professional, switching between the roles of sovereign and
friar until they finally merge. He also functions flawlessly as stage
manager by minutely programming each character's appearance and
posture. He expects both Isabella and Mariana to occupy specific
stands along the processional route. Implacement in this instance coincides with performance just as position in the sense of office and rank
had previously carried with it the expectation of a clearly defined role.[13]
As Angelo has displaced or misplaced his office, creating by his transgression a discrepancy between appearance and action, it requires a perfectly spaced spectacle to unmask him. Ironically, Vincentio compli-
ments his deputy on his "desert" in terms of the fixed and permanent

position he has so obviously failed to attain, let alone maintain:

> O, your desert speaks loud, and I should wrong it
> To lock it in the wards of covert bosom,
> When it deserves with characters of brass
> A forted residence 'gainst the tooth of time
> And razure of oblivion.
> (V.i.9–13)

The duke expresses his attitude toward his substitute's questionable merits not only in terms of a permanent place or frame but in those of textuality. He transforms Angelo's brief but ignominious administrative stint into an immortal dramatic work—into *Measure for Measure* itself. The apprehensive Angelo should, nonetheless, detect a threat in those "characters of brass," but not of gold, for they might express effrontery as well as the falseness of his own base "mettle." At this juncture, the now dramatically spaced out deputy can no longer discover a role of his own.[14]

Isabella and Mariana perform, as ordered, the role of suppliant, each, so to speak, in her niche, while the duke insists on playing the part of willful ignorance as though to elude action and retard the expected denouement. Mariana even exclaims:

> As this is true,
> Let me in safety raise me from my knees,
> Or else for ever be confixèd here
> A marble monument.
> (V.i.228–31)

If her worst fears should come true, displacement would result in a definitive placement—in its extreme form a marble monument, in every respect an invariable and unvarying spectacle that would force the play to come to a slightly premature stop. And Duke Vincentio, as soon as his two antithetical roles merge once and for all, imposes a temporary stasis by appropriating Angelo's centrally located seat on the stage: "We'll borrow place of him" (V.i.358).[15]

Angelo relinquishes his place and very nearly his existence. Isabella, assuming perhaps for the last time her habitual posture of suppliant, can do no less than plead for the deputy's pardon, and not only because she had advocated mercy during their initial confrontation. Indeed, she even points to mitigating circumstances partly justifying his transgression, namely the spectacle of her charming presence—"I partly think / A due sincerity governed his deeds, / Till he did look on me" (V.i.441–43)—thus recognizing in her own seductiveness the generating vision of Angelo's disastrous fall from grace. Mariana, in order to save her guilty husband, reverses the usual descent of love into contracts, monetary exchange, and death by transforming it into an unlikely spectacle of pure generosity. And Vincentio follows her cue in proposing marriage to a transposed but perhaps hesitant Isabella: "What's mine is yours, and what is yours is mine" (V.i.532). Will she accept his offer? Since Shakespeare has not allowed her to answer, at least in words, every director, spectator, or reader has a chance to invent a more or less convincing scenario for the "authentic" Isabella. If we rely on a theological interpretation of the play, the Christ figure Vincentio will probaby marry the Wise Virgin Isabella. But Vivian Thomas has persuasively argued that the novice shows greater concern for social than for theological issues, witness her statement to the disguised duke: "I had rather my brother die by the law, than my son should unlawfully be born" (III.i.188–90).[16] And perhaps Lucio's promptings led the heroine not only to her spirited performance in the presence of Angelo but to countenance a secular marriage. After all, when she had previously performed the part of a rigorous Clarist nun, Duke Vincentio, the supreme dramatist, had had nothing whatever to do with the assignment. Her likely change in status from cloistress to duchess may finally depend on generosity, here defined as a gift of the theater, a gift of casting. And what would prevent theology, society, and theatricality from reaching at least a provisional agreement on the level of a purely mundane performance?[17]

FIVE

Narratives of Treachery
in *Othello*

Much Ado about Nothing, Twelfth Night, and *Measure for Measure* tell their stories without undue reliance on past events. Although Don John's hatred for his brother in *Much Ado about Nothing* precedes the action of the play and accounts for many developments in the plot, we never discover or even ponder the reason for his hostility, since motivation scarcely matters. Much of the action in *Twelfth Night*'s typically romantic plot consists in freeing Olivia and Orsino from inveterate constraints out of which they will burst into a festive present. By delegating his authority in order to revive an old and almost forgotten law, Vincentio, in *Measure for Measure,* creates a crisis in the present which only his genius as a man of the theater can solve.

Tragedy as a rule overdetermines the past: in *Oedipus the King,* the protagonist painfully recovers his origins; in *Hamlet,* past events force the hero to seek revenge; in *Phèdre,* everything ties in with the heroine's heredity and Venus's persistent persecution of her family; in *Athalie,* an alien queen runs afoul of God's long-standing promise to his chosen people. Although past actions in *Othello* in no way coincide with fate, they nonetheless dominate the entire work in a most peculiar and elusive manner, perhaps because of the lack of a standard tragic plot based on hidden transgressions. After everybody's safe arrival in Cyprus and Cassio's alcoholic bout, no new event occurs until the end, for we attend mainly questionable narratives and distorting dialogues recounting fabricated happenings; and although the tragedy features a triumphant general, heroic action emerges only as fictional narratives based on adventures that preceded the actual drama. In the fugal interplay between illusion and elusion, the building up of the plot relies more often than not on lies—illusions in the ordinary sense—while elusion somehow leads to the reduction if not the disappearance of the momentous acts expected in a tragedy.

We cannot regard *Othello* as lacking in metadramatic subtlety, even though it can hardly rival *Measure for Measure* and *Hamlet* in this respect. The performative aspects of the play, however, do pose a certain number of thorny problems not encountered elsewhere. Once the wellspring of heroic action has dried up, Othello and the other warriors, having in a sense lost their purpose, fall back on the provisional roles imposed by a peaceful and domesticated universe. Unlike the victorious soldiers in *Much Ado about Nothing*, Othello the married man need no longer indulge in amorous or even courtly pursuits. Having left his legendary past behind him and without any heroic enterprise in sight, he has reduced himself to the vulnerable stasis of his presence on stage. Indeed, the cleavage in action happens to coincide with an insuperable gap between his stage appearance and his accomplishments. And rifts appear everywhere, for instance, in the discrepancy between a tragic outcome and a perversely debased causality, tantamount at times to a diabolically farcical intrigue. Moreover, the division in action coincides with a discrepancy in discourse. Othello's epic eloquence, a carryover from his leadership in war, clashes with Iago's demeaning satirical innuendo. In both word and action, the characters in the play become victims of their assigned but, under present circumstances, deactivated and suspended roles, revealing perhaps that not one of them, with the exception of Desdemona, has sufficient integrity to live up to and perform in accordance with his or her original casting.

Classicists, even those who profess to admire Shakespeare as man of the theater, poet, philosopher, and psychologist, merely frown on his deliberate neglect of the unities, while condemning outright his propensity to introduce comic gaps and, worse still, bawdy interludes into his tragedies.[1] Paradoxically, *Othello,* the most tightly knit and, hence, most "classical" of his tragedies, appropriates comic techniques and uses irony more than any other of his serious dramas. And like many a classical tragedy, it relies, as so many scholars have noted, on narrated scenes. John Bayley has explored the abundant generic contrasts and interweavings that mark the play, and Susan Snyder has shown how tragedy develops from "a questioning of comic assumptions."[2] It appears, at least on the surface, that a condottiere, who owes his lofty position as governor of Cyprus to his skillful stategy in war and his ability as organizer, succumbs with all the aplomb of a senescent gull to commedia dell'arte tactics. We generally expect that a tragic figure will come to grief in the lofty manner of Oedipus and Phèdre, victims of a supernatural power, or like Lear and Macbeth because of a weakness or perversity threatening the very existence of the state. Surprisingly, Othello's downfall begins only after a gigantic storm has secured the coasts of Cyprus for years to come by conveniently smashing a Turkish armada.[3] Thus the general's destruction becomes little more than a domestic matter entailing, from the standpoint of the state, his questionable but routine replacement by Cassio. Shakespeare, if he had so wished, could have set his protagonist's turmoil within the framework of a Turkish invasion of the island. But in that case he might have had to upgrade stylistically Iago's part as manipulating villain to the potentially more menacing role of traitor. It would seem that in thus dealing with mainly private matters, Shakespeare wisely resorted to devices generically associated with a comedy such as Ben Jonson's *Volpone,* which ends so dismally for most of the characters involved. For that reason, one might in some respects classify the play as a domestic tragedy.[4]

Apart from his jealousy, arguably a new and unexpected development in his career, Othello does not appear to suffer from the kind of flaw—pride, vanity, ambition, unrequited passion—that so frequently makes a protagonist vulnerable.[5] Nor has he betrayed the state or usurped power to attain his ends. Scrupulously faithful to the "most potent, grave, and reverend signiors" (I.iii.76), he wishes for nothing better than the responsible and merited post he has attained as leader of the armed forces of Venice, a position climaxed by his elopement with a senator's daughter. Successful in love and war, he has attained through legitimate means every one of his goals. And he discovers on his way to the island that instead of another enemy to vanquish, he has only a friendly people to please with the help of the winning woman who adores him. Reunited with her upon his auspicious arrival in Cyprus, he has at long last fulfilled his fondest ambitions. Unfortunately, he cannot sufficiently identify with his past achievements or with the heroic image he has indelibly imposed upon Desdemona to preserve his legendary glory. Because of disproportions between causes and effects, between means and results, the reversal of his fortunes can readily compare with that of any other tragic protagonist, including Oedipus.

The Moor suffers from no other weakness than a strange discrepancy within himself, which makes him highly vulnerable to the first enemy clever and evil enough to take advantage of this corroded chink in his armor. Even before Othello has a chance to make his initial appearance on stage, the words of Iago, Roderigo, and Brabantio reveal a gap between his heroic reputation as a warrior and his perceived identity. By identity I mean his stage presence, if not his casting, as a fearsome black barbarian. Early in the play, Iago sums up in a cruel pun the cleavage besetting his commanding officer: "His Moorship" (I.i.33), which explosively brings out the inherent contradiction between rank and visibility: explosive, because Iago in this tone-setting witticism approximates the jack-in-the-box technique defined and analyzed by Henri Bergson.[6] "His Worship" cannot prevent the Moor from stubbornly rearing his awesome countenance and proclaiming his alien origins. Although most Venetian aristocrats consider the formidable warrior indispensable to the state, very few indeed would countenance him as a member of their family. Brabantio, who had regularly invited the conquering general to his palazzo, panics upon discovering the Moor's tryst with Desdemona. Now, Othello could easily cope with such ambivalent attitudes toward his person if he did not happen to share them; and his failure to separate his lofty casting from his private image will lead to his downfall. Since he does not despite his splendid achievements fully believe in himself, how could he possibly trust Desdemona, in whom he apparently sees Venice incarnate—that civilized other that stamps him as an outsider?

Iago, the very antithesis of Desdemona, pushes division and displacement even further than does his master. Costumed in telltale black on the Jacobean stage, he tirelessly points to himself as villain, in contrast to his frequently reiterated designation by other characters as "honest." Thus his stage presence constantly belies his undeserved reputation. Behaving in this respect like the scheming protagonist of a comedy, he helpfully informs the audience of his sinister schemes while his onstage victims, convinced of his honesty, remain in the dark. But Iago, who appears to derive in equal measure from the knaves of Roman and Italian farce and from the devils and vices of the medieval stage, gives evidence of still another rift.[7] Aide-de-camp of the generalissimo and seemingly third in command of the Venetian forces in Cyprus, he functions mainly as the trusted factotum and servant of the Moor, thus accepting the humble tasks of an orderly while strongly resenting the inexperienced Cassio's unwarranted preferment. Although he behaves in the manner of the enterprising servants of ancient comedy, notably in his parasitical relationship with Roderigo, he feels that Othello should have recommended him for, and the Senate appointed him to, the post of lieutenant. He thus must remain an "ancient," a term that in Elizabethan slang meant procurer, a role he eagerly plays in gulling Roderigo, whom he pretends to help in the seduction of Desdemona.[8] Emilia, the heroine's lady-in-waiting and bosom companion, belies her rank by performing the tasks of chambermaid in the Moor's household. Desdemona orders her, "Give me my nightly wearing" (IV.iii.15); Emilia states, "I have laid those sheets you bade me on the bed" (21), and asks, "Shall I go fetch your nightgown?" (33), to which her mistress replies, "No, unpin me here" (34). Although Emilia in accomplishing her domestic duties unknowingly prepares her mistress— and indeed herself—for death, thus intensifying the poignancy of the scene, her behavior nevertheless adds just another discrepancy and disproportion to the play. We indeed see Emilia and Iago constantly playing demeaning, contradictory, and even clashing roles, thus revealing their inability or perhaps their unwillingness to perform in a manner befitting their rank. The presence of sheets and a nightgown as well as the fuss made about a purloined handkerchief shocked the Parisian audience attending the first run of Alfred de Vigny's translation of *Othello*.[9] In spite of the leveling effect of their Revolution, the classical French hardly relished such unwonted interminglings of genres and classes. But their cultural shock does draw attention to some of the disquieting features of the tragedy. Cassio's metamorphosis from perfect gentleman to brute after one drink too many may have appeared no less unwarranted to the French audience even though it conforms to the movement of a play featuring repeated reversals in behavior.

The unwonted performative behavior of the various characters correlates with their preferences in style. Here again a brief comparison with French classicism may help bring out some of the puzzling stylistic qualities and performative clues in *Othello*. The characters in any tragedy of Racine, whatever their rank or the intensity of their emotions, invariably speak a dignified, elevated, usually poetic, and somewhat abstract language that nevertheless does not preclude variety or flexibility even if it does exclude the naming of bed linen, nighties, and kerchiefs as well as the deliberate use of sexual equivocation. In short, Racine insists on maintaining tonal continuity throughout as though to echo the unities of action, place, and time. Shakespeare on the contrary prefers the tonal discontinuities of clashing styles, running the gamut from "honest" satire through euphuistic lyricism to high epic. Iago, for obvious reasons, favors low and debasing satire; Othello, in conformity with past military prowess, prefers the epic; Cassio, a well-bred Florentine gentleman, indulges whenever he can in précieux hyperbole; the sententious duke and Brabantio resort to rhyming proverbs or truisms, for instance: "To mourn a mischief that is past and gone / Is the next way to draw new mischief on" (I.iii.204–5). Variations in linguistic expression, however, have an even more important function than the delineation of rank, age, or character. In this regard, Shakespeare has only partially anticipated Buffon's famous but usually misquoted statement "Le style est de l'homme même" (style reveals the man), for in *Othello* style frequently takes precedence over character and, so to speak, performatively upstages it. Indeed, the play features a war between generically antithetical styles which foregrounds the dramatic conflicts between opposing individuals or principles. Moreover, it self-consciously exploits by means of language the gap and displacement, inevitable in the theater, between representation and perception. Past events show that Iago has every reason to resent Cassio and hate a master who, in his opinion, has betrayed him, if not, as he suspects, by seducing his wife, at least by preventing his advancement. It would seem, however, that story line matters less here than do generic oppositions. Iago, Othello, and Cassio hardly conform in their manner of speech to the type of discourse expected of characters in a tragedy—for instance of Caesar, Brutus, Macbeth, Macduff, and Lear, let alone Oedipus, Antigone, Phèdre, and Athalie. Such deviation from usual practice has much less to do with lack of elevation than with generic displacement, for we can hardly accuse Othello or Cassio of favoring a low style, even though the Moor sounds more and more like Iago as the play progresses, only to revert to his former speech habits late in the play.[10]

Iago, as I have already suggested, shows a marked penchant for satire, the medium best suited to his role as knave in both senses of the word. Now satire, by its insistence on frankness and realism, appears far more truthful and "honest" than other poetic modes; and the villain by frequently using it in conjunction with his shrewd analysis and jaundiced view of human conduct provides satire with a corroborative if not an objective correlative. Shakespeare has endowed his villain with remarkable if deliberately specialized poetic gifts; his satirical vein rivals Othello's mastery of the epic and far surpasses Cassio's conventional lyricism. In any case, it enables him to upstage the Moor during most of the play, marked by a progressive degradation of the epic mode.[11] In revealing Desdemona's elopement, Iago felicitously combines sustained metaphor with alliteration ("you'll have your daughter covered with a Barbary horse, you'll have your nephews neigh to you; you'll have coursers for cousins, and gennets for germans" [I.i.111–13]), all the while mocking the senator, disparaging the general, and making a true if distorted statement about the event. He could of course have told Brabantio quite simply that his daughter had eloped and married the Moor; Cassio could no doubt have supplied an ecstatic epithalamium for the occasion; and we will soon hear Othello's epic "dilations."[12]

Iago shows so much imagination in recounting Cassio's spectacular but trumped-up dream that his graphic narrative verges on the incredible:

> "Sweet Desdemona,
> Let us be wary, let us hide our loves!"
> And then sir, would he gripe and wring my hand,
> Cry, "O sweet creature!" and then kiss me hard,
> As if he plucked up kisses by the roots
> That grew upon my lips; then laid his leg
> Over my thigh, and sighed, and kissed, and then
> Cried "Cursed fate that gave thee to the Moor!"
>   (III.iii.419–26)

In providing the only graphic account of Desdemona's alleged infidelity, Iago casts himself in the dual role of audience and reluctant participant.[13] In bearing false witness, he cannot resist giving free play to his satirical and grotesque vein; he pushes theatricality to such an absurd extreme that he provides the dreamer with a full-blown scenario, wherein poor Cassio, substituting his unlikely bedfellow for chaste and beautiful Desdemona, demonstrates in words and gesture his carnal passion. Moreover, Iago has succeeded in creating a performable scene that belongs, when taken out of context, to bawdy farce, but that his victim inevitably sees in a sinister light and that the offstage audience views with considerable foreboding. In his preamble, the villain took care to situate Cassio's alleged outpourings within a universal psychological framework: "There are a kind of men so loose of soul, / That in their sleeps will mutter their affairs. / One of this kind is Cassio" (III.iii.416–18). And this quasi-syllogistic preamble lends an air of credibility to an unbelievable tale worthy of Boccaccio. In a sense, Iago in his narrative reveals more than meets the eye, for by substituting his own person for that of Desdemona he actually points to the origins of her alleged betrayal and by resorting to a dream he shows the illusory source of his accusations. This detailed narrative, by implicating its perpetrator, provides just another instance of Iago's persistent and self-designating performance as villainous liar. Beneath the surface, he reveals all Othello should know, but will discover much too late, about his ancient's activities as performer and dramatist.

In his burlesque scenario, Desdemona figures as a debased object of desire. By recasting her in the role best suited to his own literary style, the villain has removed her from the pedestal on which her epic and idealizing husband had placed her.[14] Instead of the heroine he had created, if not in his own image, at least in the semblance of his lofty narratives— "O my fair warrior!" (II.i.180)—the Moor now pictures a strumpet eager to satisfy an adulterer's outspoken desires.

In order to win her hand, Othello had narrated his deeds in an epic style perfectly suited to intertextual adventures deriving from the *Odyssey,* the *Illiad,* and embroidered accounts by explorers of exotic lands. Whether or not he had given Desdemona a faithful account, he had verbally transformed his life into fiction. In his attempt to reassure Roderigo, Iago can, with a shade of plausibility, accuse his master of telling deliberate lies: "Mark me with what violence she first loved the Moor, but for bragging and telling her fantastical lies; and will she love him still for prating? Let not thy discreet heart think it. Her eye must be fed; and what delight shall she have to look on the devil?" (II.i.220–24). Iago's account of the winning of Desdemona actually repeats on a satirical level Othello's persuasive speech before the duke. Moreover, the villain pointedly reveals, as though the audience had not already noticed it, the cleavage between the conquering general's fictional representations and his visible image or stage presence.

In his speech before the "Most potent, grave, and reverend signiors" (I.iii.76), Othello had needed only to summarize his lengthy narratives in order to explain Desdemona's enthusiastic reception of them. The young woman had indeed provided him with the most favorable audience any author, including Shakespeare himself, could wish for. Her passionate reaction to fiction outstrips the dedication to novels of Don Quixote, of Molière's adolescent précieuses, and of Emma Bovary, none of whom actually enjoyed the intimate presence of their favorite storyteller. The general's literary performance unfortunately meets with harsh and disparaging criticism on the part of his ancient. It would seem that the dramatist has built into his play two extreme forms of audience response, capable of framing all possible judgments, positive or negative, that the public might form about his protagonist.

Upon hearing his persuasive defense, the "signiors" must see the Moor through the appreciative eyes of Desdemona. In spite of his modest disclaimer, "Rude am I in my speech" (I.iii.81), he has clearly mastered the verbal art of manipulating an audience:

> My story being done,
> She gave me for my pains a world of sighs.
> She swore, i' faith, 'twas strange, 'twas passing strange;
> 'Twas pitiful, 'twas wondrous pitiful.
> She wish'd she had not heard it; yet she wished
> That heaven had made her such a man. She thanked me;
> And bade me, if I had a friend that loved her,
> I should but teach him how to tell my story,
> And that would woo her. Upon this hint I spake.
> She loved me for the dangers I had passed,
> And I loved her that she did pity them.
> This only is the witchcraft I have used.
>   (I.iii.158–69)

If we can trust his narrated account of Desdemona's cumulative response to protracted "dilations," it would appear that the Moor has momentarily narrowed but not quite closed the gap separating his legend, in the etymological sense of the term, from his stage presence. He does not seem to fear at that moment that by confusing wooing with storytelling Desdemona may have welcomed him in place of a more legitimate suitor—of some hypothetical fair-haired Venitian friend who would repeat his adventures. In short, by attributing his success as wooer not to himself but to his stories he leaves himself open to a reversal, for he implies in his speech to the "signiors" that Desdemona may have loved him less for himself than for his narrated adventures. The duke, no doubt a man of words, has no misgivings whatever, for he exclaims, "I think this tale would win my daughter too" (I.iii.171). More important still, Othello situates the winning of Desdemona within a performative framework that would have overwhelmed Aristotle, for fear and pity lead not only to catharsis but to a wedding. As Othello has fallen in love with an audience and as Desdemona has become enamored of the performative telling of a tale, their reciprocated passion snugly fits into a theatrical setting. And the way of telling a story appears to have mattered no less to Desdemona than its actual content or veracity (see I.iii.164–65). In short, she shows an inordinate weakness for performative expressiveness in literature, whereby rhetoric can produce all the effects Brabantio had attributed to witchcraft. But some of the most eloquent among the church fathers had viewed rhetoric with considerable suspicion as a diabolical invention. In any case, Desdemona's response shows at the very least that Othello's so-called rude speech has through epic discourse led to romance.

After the Moor has fallen under Iago's reductive spell to the point of imitating the villain's manner of speech, he nonetheless harks back with a poignant show of nostalgia to the epic behavior and style he must forever forsake:

> O, now for ever
> Farewell the tranquil mind! farewell content!
> Farewell the plumèd troop, and the big wars
> That makes ambition virtue! O, farewell!
> Farewell the neighing steed and the shrill trump,
> The spirit-stirring drum, th' ear-piercing fife,
> The royal banner, and all quality,
> Pride, pomp, and circumstance of glorious war!
> And O you mortal engines whose rude throats
> Th' immortal Jove's dread clamors counterfeit,
> Farewell! Othello's occupation's gone!
>   (III.iii.347–56)

His warlike occupation must vanish with this final surge of his epic style, a surge marked by spectacular images and sound effects contrasting with the pathetic style that will prevail during Desdemona's muted murder. Initially, his prowesses had dilated into heroic discourse; but now that he sees his wife as an unworthy and unappreciative audience, he paradoxically must fail to find the way back from verbal performance to heroic action. Narrative has become for him a headlong flight with little chance of returning to past glories. Desdemona's alleged betrayal has reduced him to his pathetic but menacing presence on the stage where he now stands, a hero separated from his legendary deeds and without hope for a future. A prisoner of his own and of Iago's fictions, he has fallen into the verbal web he had so patiently spun for Desdemona.[15]

By transforming his life from boyhood to the present into a series of fictional narratives, he has facilitated and almost assured the triumph of Iago. As a man of action—if only the Turkish armada had not met with disaster!—he would no doubt have remained far less vulnerable, for the villain exerts his corrosive mastery mainly over words; but as the hero of a story—albeit his own—the Moor has not only left himself far more open than Duke Vincentio to the inventions of others, but he has lost faith in his own irremediably fictionalized career. He must henceforth function as the groping reader and critic of his own legendary script, which still includes Desdemona. No less intertextual in his approach than his chief, Iago enjoys the relatively simple task of rewriting and interpolating trite but demeaning texts as so many sequels to Othello's already fictionalized existence. The latter's apparently triumphant tales have, with Iago's help, served only to widen the gap between heroic image and presence, as his fivefold repetition of "farewell" would seem to imply. And these admirable fables have actually initiated a betrayal that the villain's lies will eagerly complete.

Unlike Othello and Iago, the faithful Cassio has little use for fiction and shows only minimal talent as a dramatist. He makes up to a slight extent for these shortcomings by a verbal dexterity that serves to heighten events without in any way changing them. He therefore has very little impact on the unfolding of the tragedy apart from the role he unwittingly plays in Iago's scenario. One might even claim that during the early stages of the play his euphuistic lyricism provides a high-pitched accompaniment to, if not a weak echo of, the Moor's thundering voice. The Florentine gentleman reacts most appropriately to the news of Desdemona's safe arrival in Cyprus:

> Tempests themselves, high seas, and howling winds,
> The guttered rocks and congregated sands,
> Traitors ensteeped to clog the guiltless keel,
> As having sense of beauty, do omit
> Their mortal natures, letting go safely by
> The divine Desdemona.
>
> (II.i.68–73)

In his fragmentary ode, Cassio makes good use of hyperbole and personification as though to point out that nature in its most treach-
erous aspects ironically behaves far more kindly toward beauty than
will Iago and Othello. Although Cassio unwittingly adheres to the
thematics of a play emphasizing the perils of betrayal, his encomium
of a still-absent Desdemona appears singularly inappropriate because the poetic clichés involved have so little to do from a stylistic
point of view with the language of serious drama. Précieux verse of
this type would more readily fit into a comedy featuring among other
stock characters a militant poetaster in search of occasions to show
off his verse. But the deliberate inappropriateness of the clichés suits
the dramatist's purpose, for it provides an additional but hardly
threatening discrepancy between action and rhetoric consonant with
the lieutenant's peculiar presence in the play. He hovers most of the
time at the periphery of action, desperately wanting in, until the Senate ironically places him at center stage after the tragedy has nearly
run its course.

Cassio had previously managed to praise the same Desdemona in
an impeccably courtly manner:

> He hath achieved a maid
> That paragons description and wild fame;
> One that excels the quirks of blazoning pens,
> And in th' essential vesture of creation
> Does tire the ingener.
> (II.i.61–65)

Like many a skilled versifier before him, the Florentine aristocrat
scales the heights of hyperbole by proclaiming the incapacity of
words to do justice to the lady's ineffable perfections. Iago will soon
use a less elevated style and rhetoric to convince Othello of the same
lady's irremediable imperfection. Both the lieutenant in his fulsome
praise and the ancient in his disparagement deliberately practice reductive methods, for their rhetoric has little to do with Desdemona's
actual stage presence. Like them, Othello, in his jealousy if not in his
love, will misinterpret, by words and unfortunately by deeds, the behavior of his wife. Desdemona, whatever she does or says, invariably
meets with misunderstanding even if she always speaks clearly and

reasonably without attempting rhetorical flights. We can accuse only the male characters of twisting language to suit their self-defeating purpose.

In spite of the many comic, satirical, trivial, and even farcical elements that emerge throughout the play, despite numerous variations and jumps in style, *Othello* stands out as one of the starkest dramas ever performed and Iago as one of the most sinister scoundrels in all theater. Perhaps the clash between Iago's satirical vein and the Moor's elevated style leads to tragedy in the same way that apparently insignificant incidents trigger the main peripeteia of the play and bring about the catastrophe. In short, apparently feeble causes, linguistic or other, produce disproportionate effects. But usually such discrepancies or disproportions between cause and effect produce, as Henri Bergson has shown, laughter rather than fear and pity.[16] And as two of the main features of the plot—an elopement and a jealous husband—traditionally belong to comedy, it would seem that Shakespeare has produced tragedy by systematically undermining the epic. In fact, the epic, already breached by Iago and Roderigo in the opening scene, loses all purpose after the destruction of the Turkish fleet. As in *King Lear,* the "storm within" easily replaces external threats; and the Moor's inner turmoil can substitute for the epic fury that a Turkish invasion of Cyprus would have wrought. Here again, displacement and disproportion play an important part by focusing the Moor's belligerence not on a powerful opponent but on a loving and defenseless victim. In the place of naked swords and cutlasses, deceptive language inflicts mortal wounds; and in keeping with this substitution, Othello murders Desdemona by smothering and silencing her with that most unwarlike of weapons, a pillow, which, like the handkerchief, belongs to a purely domestic world. We might claim in this connection that the Moor's irretrievable act consisted in bringing by means of narrative his epic existence into a Venetian parlor, in the etymological sense of that term. This initial transfer, by reducing a hero's life to a tale, opens the way to more perilous divisions, and Iago requires only generic and stylistic substitutions to undo a vulnerable master. Nevertheless, the carryover from the epic somehow transposes and upgrades Iago's commedia dell'arte tricks to make them serve the purpose of tragedy, for we see the dismal spectacle of a powerful and apparently secure leader succumbing to patently fabricated delusions. As a result, Emilia's insults—"coxcomb," "gull," "fool"—compound Othello's tragic predicament by tearing off the last shreds of his heroic persona.

To become a tragic figure, Othello actually requires the baseness of the character who plots his downfall as well as the insignificance of the narrated or performed incidents that mislead him and of the props—handkerchief, nightgown, sheets, pillow—that play an essential part in, or accompany, Desdemona's murder. Othello's tragedy consists in his unrelenting reduction from his preliminary casting as successful and almost legendary warrior to his final employment as gull and bogeyman. Iago has gradually brought down a legend to his own level, and not only in speech; even in his suicide, Othello resorts to a device reminiscent of Iago's habitual trickery. The Moor narrates for the last time one of his real or imaginary adventures so as to divert his attentive guardians, and at the climax of the story he stabs himself: "I took by th' throat the circumcisèd dog, / And smote him—thus" (V.ii.355–56).[17] Lodovico underscores the close connection between action and narrative by exclaiming, "O bloody period!" (V.ii.357), and Gratiano adds, "All that is spoke is marr'd." As a preamble to his final speech, Othello, a spinner and victim of fables, had movingly but somewhat ironically insisted that his listeners tell the truth in their report:

> I pray you, in your letters,
> When you shall these unlucky deeds relate,
> Speak of me as I am. Nothing extenuate,
> Nor set down aught in malice. Then you must speak
> Of one that loved not wisely, but too well.
> (V.ii.340–44)

He seems to insist on dictating their report, for he commands, "Set you down this" (V.ii.351). We shall never know whether or not his listeners obediently wrote the whole truth and nothing but the truth in their letters or whether they copied Shakespeare's script. In any case, the denouement focuses on the questionable nature of narrative, seen here as a fatal imposture, as though to provide final confirmation of the dangerous influence it had exerted since the beginning.

Among the various props attendant upon the undoing of Desdemona, the handkerchief stands out as by far the most important. Several critics, notably Jean Dubu in a recent article, have seen in it far more than an insignificant if richly embroidered domestic object whose disappearance and subsequent reappearance lead to the downfall of Desdemona.[18] For the Moor and his wife, it has at the very least the sentimental value of a first gift; and for this reason Desdemona expresses bitter regret at its loss. More important still, narrative confers on it occult powers out of proportion with its ornate appearance and especially with its humble domestic function. For this reason, this woven and embroidered texture repeats in its own way the cleavage that divides Othello while providing a symbolic summary of the entire tragic text. Desdemona's—and the audience's—information concerning its so-called occult powers, however, comes from the Moor himself and thus functions as just another narrative told by an inveterate and presently untrustworthy storyteller:

> Make it a darling like your precious eye.
> To los't or giv't away were such perdition
> As nothing else could match.
> DES. Is 't possible?
> OTH. 'Tis true. There's magic in the web of it.
> A sibyl that had numb'red in the world
> The sun to course two hundred compasses,
> In her prophetic fury sewed the work;
> The worms were hallowed that did breed the silk;
> And it was dyed in mummy which the skillful
> Conserved of maidens' hearts.
> (III.iv.66–75)

No wonder that with a handkerchief containing such potent ingredients Othello's mother could charm and subdue her husband. By asking "Is 't possible?" and "I' faith is 't true?" (III.iv.76), Desdemona may express more doubt than astonishment, for until that moment strong magic had played little if any part in her relationship with Othello. In fact, fiction had until then sufficed for every occasion. But we may doubt that the general himself believes in the veracity of his own narrative. He may very well have invented the story on the spur of the moment just to terrorize his wife, for if true the tale would confirm Brabantio's worst suspicions about the Moor's use of black magic in seducing his daughter. It would therefore seem likely that Othello has sarcastically invented a tall story deliberately modeled on Brabantio's false perception of him. By means of this imaginative but incredible narrative, he thus puts Desdemona squarely in the enemy camp. He sardonically transforms himself into the black barbarian, capable of commiting unmentionable crimes, whom Venetians have had good reason to mistrust and would never welcome into their families. According to this essentially performative interpretation, Othello's story would deserve little more credence than Iago's account of Cassio's dream. Once again the Moor may have imitated the villain's contrived performance. In his relationship with Desdemona, he has moved from fictions based at least in part on true adventures to utter fabrication. He has drifted into a web of untruth originating in his own narrations but presently aided and abetted by Iago's sinister lies to which he responds with impostures of his own invention. Fictional discourse stands out as even more dangerous than the villain, who without the eminently theatrical separation between stage presence and persona might never have found a way to destroy his master.

SIX

Hamlet: Actor,
Student Prince,
and Avenger

Whereas in *Othello, the Moor of Venice,* the hero, in his failure to identify with past glories, undermined and displaced by fiction, succumbs to a stage presence clearly programmed in the title, the protagonist of *Hamlet, Prince of Denmark* succeeds during five long acts in protracting and enhancing his spectacular stage presence instead of hurrying to complete the indispensable action demanded by his father and awaited by the audience. It would thus appear that Shakespeare has deliberately miscast these two characters in opposite ways. The conquering general can no longer live up to his billing; and the dashing prince behaves as though he regarded the trite role of avenger as a slur and blemish on his stage presence, geared to highly sophisticated and intellectual performances. While retelling how a brave prince, after many a delay, finally punished his father's heinous assassin, the tragedy recounts the hidden struggle between an imaginary dramatist, compelled to move his plot along, and a star performer, dissatisfied with his assignment, who reluctantly consents to participate in the action, but only on his own terms. Shakespeare not only provides a superlative example of the fugal interplay between illusion and elusion, but he widens almost to the breaking point the gap between the two, so much so that the plot perversely appears to unravel at the slightest provocation. Pirandello never went any further in deconstructing the stage than Shakespeare in *Hamlet.* As we might expect, the unraveling of the plot and the hero's compulsion to distance himself from the blood and thunder expedients of a typical revenge play depend on an overdetermination of language, quite different from the overdetermination of discourse prevalent in *Othello*.

Words and Indirection

This overdetermination of language manifests itself first of all quantitatively. *Hamlet* clearly stands out as Shakespeare's longest play; and the prince, both in the number of lines he speaks and their ratio to the total length of the tragedy, verbalizes far more than any other Shakespearean protagonist.[1] No one has a better right to exclaim, "Words, words, words" (II.ii.191), both as speaker and as reader. Within the play, the garrulous Polonius comes in third, behind the scheming villain Claudius, who has some 540 lines to his credit. Among major masterpieces of the stage, only Molière's hyperactive Scapin, who rarely delays the action, exceeds the prince's remarkable output.

Perhaps the profundity and poetic style of Hamlet's speeches, or, better still, their theatrical suitability preserves him from appearing verbose even in his soliloquies. We may indeed scoff at the lord chamberlain's windy moralizing, but we always take the prince, who rarely hesitates to preach, most seriously, all the more so because, as spectators or readers, we remain steadfastly on his side even while we attempt to sound the depths of his philosophy or complexes. Polonius, on the contrary, never departs from the wisdom of the ages or expresses a sentiment that might surprise, let alone shock, his listeners. Despite his status and his purported political acumen, he appears to have at the very least a nodding acquaintance with the senile pedants of Italian comedy. Moreover, Hamlet, who invariably gives the impression of improvising and inventing, tends to react, rather than plot a course of action in the manner of King Claudius or young Fortinbras, who, having little use for words, fittingly reaps the rewards.

The unwonted wordiness of *Hamlet* should hardly astonish us, granted the high quotient of scholars, in both senses of the term, among the dramatis personae: the prince, Horatio, Laertes, Rosenkrantz and Guildenstern, with Polonius preempting the part of ar-

chetypal alumnus. Hamlet, a far more dedicated intellectual than his
fellow students, experiences as great a difficulty in holding his tongue
as the players in refraining from telling all. That he should have remained a student at the age of thirty must have seemed odd to an
Elizabethan audience, aware that mostly teenagers attended and
graduated from Oxford and Cambridge. A crown prince, once he
had attained his majority, would have seemed dreadfully out of
place, even in Wittenberg. Apart from the First Clown's precisions
concerning the hero's advanced years (V.i.137–39 and V.i.151–52),
however, everything suggests that Hamlet may not have reached his
twentieth birthday. As John W. Draper has surmised, the actor, no
doubt Richard Burbage, playing the part of Hamlet rather than the
character may have reached in 1604, date of the Second Quarto, the
age of thirty.[2] Shakespeare, in thus playing games with his audience,
would have widened the initial gap between text and performance
while adding still another instance of displacement, so characteristic
of the play.[3] In any case, it takes a direct order from the king to prevent Hamlet from resuming his studies at Wittenberg, which, by
means of a pun, becomes the prototype of all seats of learning, including Luther's alma mater.[4]

Unlike Shakespeare's sophisticated protagonist, the original
Hamlet, or Amleth, a mere child who must play the fool to save his
life, never has the chance or even the inclination to become a scholar.
Indeed, he belongs to a rather barbaric society, where only a few
clerics have learned how to read and write. Obviously, Shakespeare
has upgraded the legendary tale, both intellectually and politically—
the kingdom of Denmark replaces a mere principality. And the term
'upgrading' hardly does justice to Shakespeare's radical transformation of a rudimentary society into a polished and corrupt modern
state or to the disruption, if not the complete reversal, of the situation
described by Saxo Grammaticus in his *Historia Danica* (1514) and
Belleforest in his *Histoires tragiques* (1576). Only the inset mention-
ing the single combat between the kings of Denmark and Norway
shows traces of a feudal past. Moreover, by increasing Hamlet's age,
the dramatist had to make Gertrude considerably older than Amleth's mother, thus putting her, as her son pointedly remarks, at a season when "The hey-day of the blood is tame" (III.iv.69). In short,

Shakespeare in modernizing the legendary events has sacrificed the obvious advantages of a traditional revenge plot in order to attain to a highly sophisticated theatricality based far more on indirection than on immediacy.

The predominance of a wordy intellectuality in the tragedy militates more than any other factor against dramatic directness. Paradoxically, the author waxes more sententious and philosophical than in any of his other plays, even though he deals with a subject that would seem to preclude little else than violent action. We might perhaps explain this discrepancy between subject matter and treatment in light of the unusual spectators the Globe players sought to entertain. *Hamlet* may indeed have received some of its earliest performances at Oxford and Cambridge. A typical revenge play, always full of sound and fury even in its time delaying peripeteia, would scarcely have impressed a university audience. *Hamlet* certainly owes more to Seneca than do the earlier *Romeo and Juliet* and even *Julius Caesar,* particularly in the Aeneas and Gonzago episodes. In addition to these two classical and already stylistically unfashionable inserts, the play features action-retarding soliloquies and moral lectures. Without Hamlet's genius for retarding the action, the entire drama might not have needed a second act.[5] Fortinbras, whose name suggests muscular power, far from taxing his mind about the honesty of the ghost, would have dispatched the king, who throughout the play leaves himself so open to attack that he very nearly succumbs to a rebellion, fomented but hardly planned by Laertes. With the exception of the murder, the villain's devious actions take the form of indirection, an elusory approach he shares with Polonius, who uses the term, and of course with Hamlet himself, whose performance throughout the tragedy spells indirection. Avoidance of directness, however, involves far more than a devious course of action favored by various characters, for it coincides with a system of displacements and cleavages by means of which the play repeatedly appears to take stock of itself while delaying the outcome.[6]

Indirection provides the best method for discovering "truth," or, as Polonius states, it provides a useful tool to those eager to "find directions out" (II.i.66). But far from resulting in the rapid uncovering of some elusive verity capable of leading to direct and efficacious action, indirection, as the word suggests, entails at each occurrence a period of inaction. By invariably resulting in a delay, in a suspension of time, indirection becomes synonymous with elusion, while fostering the illusion of an accomplishment. More important still, indirection coincides with the method of the dramatist and, for this reason, leads to no other "truth" than that of the theater in general and of the play *Hamlet* in particular. This fugal interplay of elusion and illusion provides the semblance of a chronological frame, removed from referential time, within which the performance can persuasively unfold, even to the extent of discouraging any questioning of the causality or even the continuity of the events recounted.[7] And this frame, no less than those in *Twelfth Night* and *Measure for Measure,* repeats in another dimension the spatial construct of the stage. In any case, the performance occurring onstage remains one step removed from decisive action and, in this manner, generates a gap, which in this highly intellectual tragedy magnifies the discrepancy inherent in all representation.

Lectures and Books

Inevitably, in a Renaissance play whose protagonist favors knowledge over power, lessons, lectures, and books appear everywhere. Frequently, the moral lecture, reduced to a minimum, has the brevity of a maxim, notably in the Gonzago episode, where the Player King, parodying perhaps the outmoded formalism of sixteenth-century tragedy, expresses himself by means of moral sentences, for instance:

> Our wills and fates do so contrary run
> That our devices still are overthrown;
> Our thoughts are ours, their ends none of our own."
> (III.ii.203–5)

It would seem that the author continues to retard the action even in an insert expressly designed to precipitate events. Polonius, a delayer in speech even more than in action, has a saw ready for every occasion. Whether or not they use maxims, the major characters, with the exception of Ophelia, who by opening in her madness an insuperable gap between language and sense provides extremes of indirection, never hesitate to deliver a lecture, preferably on ethical or social behavior. Polonius cannot refrain from preaching to his children; and Laertes, the worthy son of a sententious father, almost misses the boat while telling his sister how a proper maiden should behave when harassed by a prince. The pursuing prince sermonizes more than all the other characters combined, notably when he chastizes his mother in choice, if tactless, rhetoric after having eluded his sworn duty to kill the king. Ironically, during his first appearance onstage, he had found himself on the receiving end of a lecture delivered by his hated uncle, who had just tried to justify his hasty marriage in terms of an aporic and unperformable cleavage, "With an auspicious and a dropping eye, / With mirth in funeral and with dirge in marriage" (I.ii.11–12). Considered by many critics a master of rhetoric, the king can conceptualize as sophisticatedly as anyone in the play, but with far greater deviousness. Indeed, he shows consummate skill in hypocritically developing a commonplace concerning the death of fathers.

Claudius's lecture actually sets in motion a procedure that will prevail in most of the lessons that follow, for his admonitions to his nephew serve mainly to reassert and reinforce his authority. Polonius will behave in a similar fashion toward his children, and Hamlet will go even further in coaching the players and admonishing his mother. In any case, lectures and the enforcement of authority coincide throughout the tragedy. But without the assertion of power, such lessons might have degenerated into a sort of built-in Greek chorus capable of reducing the speaker to a minimally dramatic stasis. Lessons and lectures appear, for this reason, to occupy an intermediate position between nonhortatory philosophical discourse, such as the "To be or not to be" soliloquy, and simple exchanges or commands, such as "Who's there?" "Nay, answer me. Stand and unfold yourself," which opens the tragedy, and "Go, bid the soldiers shoot," which closes it. These military commands reveal two indispensable aspects of theater: immediate observance of cues and obedience to stage directions, without which efficient performance would become impossible. The play itself, with all its conceptual and emotional profundity, must willy-nilly fit into this performative scheme that nonetheless remains inseparable from, and indeed a prisoner of, textuality. Paradoxically, the direct military imperatives that begin and end the tragedy frame a text geared primarily to indirection and frequently consisting of intellectual discourse that compounds the elusion of action. As a result, everything within this frame—actually, the entire performance—originates in a mode of discourse, consisting of speech acts, quite foreign to it. We might also define military commands as a sort of dress rehearsal for war, or at least for the direct enforcement of political power. The many moral lessons thoughout the play relate in a similar manner to the stage because of the intent to ensure a proper performance on the part of the person who must endure the lectures, which thus function in the manner of protracted speech acts.

Nearly all these lectures, while overtly dealing with moral and social conduct, derive in one way or another from aesthetic postulates and principles. Hamlet, even before his meeting with the Ghost, objects to Claudius as much for aesthetic, not to say theatrical reasons such as casting, as for moral, psychological, or political motives. His comparison between his father and his uncle as "Hyperion to a satyr" (I.ii.140) and "no more like my father / Than I to Hercules" (152–53) recurs in the lesson he inflicts upon his mother, where he opposes the majestic portrait of King Hamlet to the unprepossessing likeness of his assassin. Here as elsewhere, the prince relies on learned representations. His long, erudite comparison ends most appropriately with a rhetorical question:

> Have you eyes?
> Could you on this fair mountain leave to feed,
> And batten on this moor? Ha! have you eyes?
> (III.iv.66–68)

The lesson concludes Hamlet's attempt to direct his mother's subsequent performances in her married life with Claudius.[8]

The prince's cruel lesson to his mother, as well as the less impassioned and triter lectures delivered by Claudius, Polonius, and Laertes, derives essentially from books, classical or merely pedagogical; their number and length easily make *Hamlet* Shakespeare's most intertextual tragedy, marked by an overdetermination of scholarly attitudes. The characters have obviously read a great deal; indeed, many of the speeches and monologues paraphrase or gloss other texts. We could even claim that the various characters follow the order and procedure of actors: reading, memorization, rehearsal, and performance. When speech and even action do not originate in books, they appear nevertheless to rely on learning and training. Hamlet's counterplot, to which his unsuspecting fellow students Rosencrantz and Guildenstern fall victim, revolves around texts and learning. The prince tells Horatio, "I once did hold it, as our statists do, / A baseness to write fair, and labored much / How to forget that learning" (V.ii.33–35). Training also plays an essential part in Hamlet's fencing match with Laertes: "Since he went into France I have been in continual practice" (V.ii.199). Hamlet has carefully prepared and rehearsed for this competitive encounter: everything pertains to a learning process, akin to the memorization and rehearsal of players. The prince succumbs in the end even though he has made himself ready for all eventualities, even though he has every right to state, "The readiness is all" (V.ii.211), for he has mainly prepared himself for his death—for the inevitable outcome of an Elizabethan tragedy. In a sense, preparation and training have brought about his downfall, for by habitually treating them as valuable in themselves he cannot avoid substituting them for decisive action. As in the fencing match, they can lead only to performance—to a performance that, by a quirk of fate or, rather, the author's manipulation, enables the reluctant hero to accomplish his solemnly assigned mission. Thus, preparation by an ironic reversal creates a displacement at the very heart of the play, for it corresponds to an alleged weakness in the protagonist's character. His aesthetic bias, based on years of schooling, leads or, rather, corresponds to deficiencies that critics, who prefer moral or psychological to theatrical causality, attribute to indecisiveness and ultimately to a complex. From a purely theatrical standpoint, the prince's insistence on preparation prevents him from functioning as an effective dramatist and, hence, as a ruler.[9] A perfectionist in everything he undertakes, he spends inordinate time on rehearsal.

The overly prepared hero mirrors the texts to which he constantly returns, and he never hesitates to reduce a situation, however disturbing, to its bookish, not to say its innocuous equivalent. He behaves like a proper scholar at the very moment the Ghost reveals Claudius's crime:

Yea, from the table of my memory
I'll wipe away all trivial fond records,
All saws of books, all forms, all pressures past
That youth and observation copied there,
And thy commandment all alone shall live
Within the book and volume of my brain,
Unmixed with baser matter.
                    (I.v.98–104)

In the very act of rejecting past experience and especially past readings, the prince metaphorically reinforces his inveterate bookishness.
Instead of undergoing a radical change, he willy-nilly remains faithful to a textual identity that will surface notably in the "To be or not
to be" soliloquy and in his characteristic attempt to "catch the conscience of the king" (II.ii.591) by means of a text. In any case, the in-
tolerable event which he now consigns to memory, far from expro-
priating previous occupants, will merely appropriate the most
prominent place among other texts and, like them, will clamor, but
with far greater insistence, for interpretation, an activity better
suited to a critic than to a dramatist.[10] This compulsive textualiza-
tion of an event and indeed of his entire memory reflects and repeats
the textual nature of the play itself—a script memorized, rehearsed,
and performed.[11] It enables, besides, the fugal interplay of illusion
and elusion to reach, so early in the tragedy, a climax, for in solemnly
renouncing his henceforth inappropriate scholarly role in order to
behave like a single-minded man of action, Hamlet in his persistent
bookishness sidetracks his father's commandment and initiates the
textual upstaging of the originating revenge plot.

     In composing *Hamlet*, Shakespeare, no less bookish than his pro-
tagonist, rewrote texts by Saxo Grammaticus, François de Belleforest, and Thomas Kyd, as well as those of Seneca, Cicero, Vergil,
Horace, Montaigne, and countless others, including of course his
own plays. Hamlet traces back his origins less to Danish or Icelandic
legends than to the author's readings of the classics. As a result, the
play serves as a battlefield for conflicting origins in search of representation wherein the prince's cultural background perpetually en-
croaches on his barbaric legend. Cicero and other famous authors in-

terfere with, and misdirect, no doubt with the hero's express encouragement, his assigned role as avenger, thus providing indirections of their own. Shakespeare has contrived in this respect a thorough metamorphosis of the original Amleth for the greater benefit of intellectuality. He has indeed buried this somewhat legendary boy under an avalanche of concepts and quotations.

The hero's textual dependency shines forth in the famous soliloquy in which he appears to comment on his wish "that the Everlasting had not fixed / His canon 'gainst self-slaughter" (I.ii.131–32). Apart from this obvious connection, the monologue on suicide has little to do with Hamlet's exalted situation or even his character. Horatio, poor but noble, and therefore vulnerable to "the slings and arrows of outrageous fortune" (III.i.58) and especially to "the proud man's contumely" (71) or "The insolence of office" (73), might legitimately in an uncharacteristic moment of weakness and depression utter such discouraging thoughts. Coming from the heir apparent to a warlike state, from a Prince Charming described by Ophelia as "The glass of fashion and the mould of form, / Th' observed of all observers" (III.i.153–54), they appear, at least from a mimetic point of view, out of place. Only their poetic beauty would seem to justify their intrusion at that moment. The ideas expressed in the soliloquy derive from Cicero's rewriting of Plato.[12] As Baldwin has shown, Hamlet paraphrases a classical text according to procedures religiously followed in Elizabethan grammar schools.[13] That the prince has not invented these ideas does not in itself imply that they fail to express his point of view or the depth of his feelings. However, the First Quarto—invariably referred to as the "bad" quarto—may allow us to question the sincerity of the famous soliloquy. Claudius provides an astonishing stage direction when he exclaims: "See where he [Hamlet] comes poring upon a booke."[14] The king's remark suggests that his nephew does not really soliloquize, but either reads from a book, perhaps Cicero's *Tusculan Disputations,* or paraphrases what he has just read. Corambis—Polonius's name in the First Quarto—immediately gives stage directions to his daughter: "And here Ofelia read you on this booke, / And walk aloofe, the King shall be unseene." Ophelia's book of orizons serves as little more than a stage prop, placed in her hands not for the good of her soul but for deception. Ophelia, in this particular instance a nonreader and an acquiescent perpetrator of illusions, invites the sardonic treatment she will receive at the hands of her bookish lover. In the battle of texts she goes down to a humiliating defeat. But the lovers' friendly relationship at the Dumb Show would seem to indicate that we should not take Hamlet's unkind treatment of her or her supposed reaction too seriously. After all, she knows better than anybody else of the attempt to gull the prince. A nunnery, at least in the proper sense of the term, would ironically provide a suitable place for a respectful girl who, at her father's bidding, obediently uses a prayerbook for a prop. Shakespeare's irony goes even further than Hamlet's, for he has staged a confrontation between a submissive heroine, who must, however reluctantly, play a prescribed part, and a recalcitrant hero who reads, glosses, but hardly invents his own text. Indeed, the prince achieves his greatest success by merely changing around the names in the king's sealed order to have him put to death upon his arrival in England. As he readily admits, he copies, but he does not actually rewrite. Even in this rather special instance, he does not go beyond an existing script but merely misdirects and reverses its purpose. As author, he limits his creativity to the interpolation of a few telling lines in the Gonzago insert. Even here he does not actually invent but obediently rewrites in mannered verse the most crucial incident in the Ghost's narrative of Claudius's villainous but still silent plot. Unlike the child Amleth, he has learned and, worse still, persists in remembering too much.

Creative or not, Hamlet, the most fashionable gentleman in all of Denmark, surpasses his rivals in a variety of games, such as wordplay and swordsmanship, all of them part and parcel of his education. Like other gifted pupils, he insists on remaining at the head of the class. For this reason, he cannot refuse the fencing match with Laertes, whom he had already bested during their ostentatious verbal confrontation in Ophelia's grave. Hamlet's juvenile propensity to confound all rivals explains in part his contempt for Claudius, a ruler incapable of emulating in anything but carousing his warlike brother. Emulation, however, takes a rather special meaning in the theater, where the proper way to surpass a rival consists quite simply in upstaging him. And Hamlet, the star of the show, leaves little to chance in upstaging characters unlucky enough to share the scene with him, including so unworthy an opponent as Osric. Only the First Clown succeeds in holding his own against him, perhaps because the most edifying historical intertexts cannot quite match the gravedigger's tangible acquaintance with death. The First Clown, who so insistently points to human materiality in its most basic form, very nearly upstages the scholarly prince and, by revealing his age to the audience, the actor entrusted with the part.

The upstaging prince does not even hesitate, in the presence of Horatio and Marcellus, to put down the Ghost through the use of levity. This ghost has little to do with Danish legends but owes its existence to the tragedies of Seneca, perhaps by way of Kyd's lost version of *Hamlet*. Thus a stock character of tragedy, played, as some claim, by the author himself, assigns to the scholarly prince the unlikely part of avenger, in which employment he sees himself as hopelessly miscast: "The time is out of joint. O cursèd spite / That ever I was born to set it right!" (I.v.188–89). Fate, or rather the playwright, has cast the leading man in an undesirable and, from a sophisticated point of view, the tritest of roles. That "the time is out of joint" not only indicates that things have suddenly gone awry in the continuum of history—in the natural deaths of fathers—but also points to a gap between the hero's identity as scholar, courtier, man of fashion, and his forced assumption of a more rudimentary part, no doubt appropriate to the mindless Fortinbras or to the actor who had played the title role in Kyd's lost drama.[15]

A Man of the Theater

A perplexing and perhaps undecidable victim of his multiple origins, whether legendary and of limited scope or scholarly and universal, Hamlet can take refuge in the theater, to which he wholeheartedly belongs and which precedes and transcends all other plausible sources.[16] Upon hearing that the players from the city have just set foot in Elsinore, he for once shows enthusiasm, even though he has not yet thought of using the stage to "catch the conscience of the King" (II.ii.591); and he eagerly asks questions concerning the child actors who compete so successfully against seasoned professionals.

He greets the players like old friends and with a warmth he had not shown his school fellows Rosencrantz, Guildenstern, and even Horatio.[17] In short, he behaves as though he had discovered his long lost family in this company of professional thespians. He recites most commendably the opening lines of the stilted Aeneas narrative, but leaves the most emotional part to the First Player, who appropriately sheds real tears while tearing passion to tatters and in the process makes the prince take stock of his own predicament in purely theatrical terms. Hamlet asks himself a compounded rhetorical question: "What would he do, / Had he the motive and the cue for passion / That I have?" (II.ii.544–46). According to the prince, who holds an inordinately high opinion of the power of dramatic performance, strong and sincere acting would "Make mad the guilty, and appall the free; / Confound the ignorant, and amaze indeed / The very faculties of eyes and ears" (II.ii.548–50).

He can hardly resist describing the hyperbolic effects of such a performance in intellectual terms, thus implying that he himself would never play a part in this exaggerated manner. Indeed, he conforms throughout to an obviously more sophisticated style of acting than does the First Player, and more in keeping with the stage behavior of the urbane gentlemen who grace such comedies as *Much Ado about Nothing* and *A Midsummer Night's Dream*. But unlike the plebeian and uncritical Bottom, he would carefully pick and choose his part. More important still, Hamlet implies that by performing according to a script he could solve all his problems and put an end to corruption in Denmark. A text capable, if intensely performed, of ensuring revenge, however, would probably fall below not only the sophisticated Burbage's but Shakespeare's lofty standards. The prince's built-in failure as a player, far from hindering Burbage and his many successors, has undoubtedly enabled them to reach performative heights perhaps unattainable in a straightforward role. Hamlet clearly places the solution to all his problems within the confines of a stage and a script, just as he has metaphorically cast his resolve to avenge his father within the context or frame of a "book and volume." We can surmise that his book of memory coincides with a script, performable only if he should consent to push aside the type of role and style of acting in which he normally excels.

In his shocked acceptance of the role of avenger, Hamlet recognizes his duty and shows a due respect for hierarchy; but apart from his public display of grief, costumed or not, at court, he does not really express filial sentiments. He greatly admires his father, whose name he bears, but essentially as a model and a spectacle: "'A was a man, take him for all in all, / I shall not look upon his like again" (I.ii.187–88). In considering him the very paragon of men, the prince transforms him into an unrepeatable spectacle, gone forever from Denmark though not from the stage, for Shakespeare himself probably played the part of the Ghost. Despite this aesthetic attitude toward the murdered king, Hamlet by no means shows a paucity of filial sentiments, but it so happens that he directs them to a less worthy and competitive person, to Yorick the jester who, according to the First Clown, a specialist in such matters, had departed this world not two months, but twenty-three years earlier. In his remarks concerning this professional performer, the prince uncovers still another among his multiplicity of origins: "he hath borne me on his back a thousand times" (V.i.174) and "Here hung those lips that I have kissed I know not how oft "(V.i.176–77). Hamlet as man of the theater traces his pedigree back to Yorick, in whom we can perceive the most fundamental kind of theatrical entertainer, insofar as a jester normally operates without a stage or even a script. Even Richard Burbage could boast of his descent from a more legitimate performer, his father, James, actor and proprietor of the Blackfriars playhouse. As origin, Yorick stands at the farthest remove both from Hamlet's scholarly background and from his legendary or aristocratic antecedents, but right at the center of performance. To complicate matters, the prince has two mothers: Gertrude and his Alma Mater, rivals for his attendance.[18]

This multiple filiation of Hamlet may help us define more precisely his performative presence within the tragedy. He appears as a student prince compelled to avenge his father, but also as the actor entrusted with the star part. As a result, he conforms to and at the same time criticizes the plot and, hence, the play where he must reluctantly function as protagonist, asserting himself all the while both as matinée idol and as drama critic, capable of theorizing about the theater in general and his own part and performance in particular. In a sense, he contemplates suicide in the manner in which a prominent actor would consider forsaking a star role—both of them would eagerly bear the burden of textuality as long as they had breath enough to speak their lines.

Hamlet's theatrical predicament, based on a fundamental ambiguity—the character's awareness of belonging both to the fable and to the stage—affects in varying degrees the other participants. Even the murdered king, in order to prompt his son toward revenge, assumes for the occasion the warlike image that had so impressed his people. His performance leads, however, to a discrepancy, for he appears in middle age, yet dresses like the young warrior who some thirty years earlier had conquered the king of Norway in single combat. Perhaps, like Hamlet, the Ghost must conform to the approximate age of the actor entrusted with the part. This martial image may correspond, however, to King Hamlet's state portrait—perhaps the very one the prince contrasts with Claudius's unprepossessing appearance. The latter must always put on a false front and use "most painted words" (III.i.53), for in order to usurp the throne of Denmark and marry Gertude, he had once and for all composed a silent and evil scenario continually holding him prisoner and thus curtailing his future both as dramatist and as performer. Laertes' behavior smacks of ostentation, a theatrical fault that would have served Hamlet well if only he could have sunk to so low a performative level; the gravediggers double as clowns; Ophelia supinely follows her father's stage directions. Polonius alone, but on a much lower level, rivals Hamlet's mastery of the theater, for he too can function as director, player, critic. He too had become enamored of the stage in his student days, playing, allegedly to great applause, the star role of Julius Caesar, stabbed somewhere in the course of the play by Brutus. His erstwhile fate on the stage has indeed programmed his destiny in the present tragedy, where he must die as a stand-in for the king while playing the part of hidden spectator. Shakespeare may very well have included a revealing in joke far more humorous than the prince's pun on "Capitol" (III.ii.100), for the two Globe players entrusted with the respective parts of Hamlet and Polonius may have recently enacted Brutus and Caesar. It would dawn on Shakespeare's audience that the habitual fate of these actors has theatrically overdetermined the destiny of the characters whose parts they play. And we see that, like everything else in the theater, Polonius's death becomes just an additional repetition leading from one performance and one play to the next.[19]

Theatricality and Truth

The search for "Truth," in theme no less than plot, pervades the entire tragedy.[20] The king and with him the entire court need to know the cause of the strange behavior of the prince, who in turn chooses to verify the authenticity of the Ghost. And, of course, everyone resorts to theatrical devices in order to apprehend elusive and elusion-producing "truths." Hamlet, Claudius, and Polonius function in this connection not only as dramatists, directors, and actors, but also, and perhaps mainly, as critics who must step back and interpret correctly, on pain of death and damnation, the performances of others, thus generating a concatenation of *mises en abyme,* including the play within the play, ably discussed by many scholars. Shakespeare, in the very act of stressing "truth"—a paradoxical enterprise in an entertaining game of illusion and elusion—has admirably succeeded in rendering his chief characters puzzling. Should we consider Claudius an unmitigated villain, with no attenuating circumstances? Did Gertrude commit adultery and, worst of all, condone assassination? The prince stands out as by far the most enigmatic character, so much so that some scholars, holding perhaps too strong a belief in his existence as a person rather than as a persona, treat his madness as more genuine than feigned to the point of diagnosing it as symptomatic of an overwhelming Oedipus complex. But critics have merely continued, with deliberately undramatic but disciplined elaborations, the practical exegesis initiated by Claudius, Gertrude, and Polonius. They have all, down to the last scholar and courtier, beaten a path to the author's superlative Mousetrap, for the play *Hamlet* can scarcely contain truth in the ordinary sense, either for the characters, even when they double as spectators, or for the offstage audience. Indeed, the enigma and undecidability of the characters refers, in the final analysis, to the paradox of performative representation with its resulting overdetermination of theatricality.[21]

Knowledge for—and of—the prince consists also if not mainly in the appreciation of a performance; and the "truth" about Hamlet, about Claudius, about the Ghost, may come down to an awareness of the performative functions of the text as revealed mainly by verbal relationships. For Hamlet, knowing the "truth" entails the uncovering and verification of an event that had preceded the play: the assassination of his father. But this crime, in order to come into focus as representation, requires all the modalities of performance: thanks to the Ghost, it emerges as a dramatic narrative, and thanks to the prince it materializes first, but apparently with little effect, as a dumb show and then, by means of textual interpolation, as a sententious dialogue between Gonzago and his queen, followed by the black magic of Lucianus's monologue preceding his pouring of the poison. And Claudius's silent crime, as narrated by the Ghost and finally voiced with telling effect by the players, relates by implication to speech—to the very substance of playwriting—for the usurper has poured a deadly poison into his brother's ear.[22] The resulting rottenness in Denmark may thus have a textual origin. The king's antecedent play, which, obviously, he had never intended for public performance, has provided him not only with a crown and a queen, but also with an indelible, if at first unwritten, text capable of blasting his career and his kingdom. His crime, as I suggested earlier, has indeed deprived him of the creative freedom necessary to a successful ruler. He has forsaken that mastery over time, indispensable to a king and to a dramatist. He has become a prisoner of his own unwritten scenario, a muted mask to which *The Tragedy of Hamlet, Prince of Denmark* owes its existence and for which it provides, from the standpoint of representation rather than cause and effect, both an origin and an aftermath.

The king's criminal deed, involved, in the text of the play, with both moral and aesthetic coherence, has broken historical continuity and made a mockery of his lesson to his nephew concerning the death of fathers. His poison has "curded" more than his brother's blood, for it has corrupted the whole of nature. Not surprisingly, numerous metaphors associate Claudius with weeds, infesting the entire verbal space of the play, whereas Ophelia, seemingly the most "natural" and vulnerable character, remains inseparable from floral imagery.[23] His short reign, like Macbeth's, appears as an interregnum suggesting the brevity of a performance and generating its own compressed time. Claudius has indeed put not only "the time," but also "Time," "out of joint," initiating by his deed the delayed or suspended time of *Hamlet,* while introducing something rotten in the state of Denmark and corrupting language. His multileveled displacement has provided, in conjunction with the multiple stage set, a suitable frame for the performance of the tragedy, for he alone has made staging necessary. He seems to regret most of all the corruption of language, of the king's Danish, for this sullying has reduced him to "painted words" that he must repeat and gloss until his last breath. He has, in addition, put himself in a situation whereby he must come to terms with language in the way an artist approaches his medium. Like Shakespeare himself, he uses words artfully at the expense of "truth" and "reality" by performing with words and making words perform. We can therefore consider him, even more than the prince, an extension of the dramatist, for his damnable crime serves as a matrix for, and a mirror of, the stage's manifestations.

All the other characters follow the king's example—the example of Shakespeare. Nor can we consider the hero an exception in this respect. Even when, as in the "To be or not to be" soliloquy, he paraphrases and glosses the writings of others, he does little more than amplify the gap in words and action initiated by his hated uncle. This cleavage and displacement, which constrain Hamlet to function as a complete man of the theater, substitutes illusion and elusion for a truth and a reality presumed to prevail in the world outside the Globe while making staging not only possible but compulsory. Throughout the tragedy, an initial reversal repeats itself, for the generating crime has compounded the falsity of all representations and substituted aesthetics for ethics. Shakespeare has indeed built the ultimate Mousetrap, where all systems of knowledge and value, our own as well as those of the Renaissance, come to grief. The myopic Fortinbras remains, but so does the Globe theater.

SEVEN

Bridging the Fictional
Gap in *The Winter's Tale*

By combining, as they usually do, tragic with comic fictions, romances add several critical problems to those raised by generically simpler plays. Not only do they frequently originate in sustained fictional narratives, where the leisurely treatment of time makes a transfer to the stage somewhat awkward, but by juxtaposing incompatible elements they run the risk of losing any kind of cohesion or coherence. For this reason, the use of performative and metadramatic techniques of various kinds appears even more necessary than in other dramatic productions. Not surprisingly, Shakespeare in *The Winter's Tale* not only resorts to practically all the performative strategies treated in the previous chapters, but even adds new ones.

His romance features an array of star dramatists and performers. Leontes overwhelms us with his visions during the first half of the play; Autolycus and Perdita take turns at outperforming all the other characters during the greater part of the last two acts; Camillo on two occasions shows his mettle as a dramatist by improvising successful scenarios at crucial moments; to Paulina we owe the most impressive staging in the entire romance: Hermione's unexpected return to life or rather to the cast; and finally the shepherd's son, who bears no other name than that of Clown, sporadically entertains the audience with his own special brand of antics. In short, the romance offers an unusual abundance of shows and skits that the spectators can enjoy even without attempting to put them into context, but that critics must painstakingly relate to the rest of the work. In spite of these overtly performative aspects, verbal analysis mainly of the new critical variety will predominate once again in my own efforts to tie everything together and give performative unity to the play.

In keeping with a majority of romances and tragicomedies, *The Winter's Tale* originates in a fictional text: Robert Greene's *Pandosto: The Triumph of Time,* an incredible story, a "winter's tale" indeed, told by an omniscient and euphuistic narrator, in which Fortune rather than Time emerges victorious. Fictional omniscience and timing undergo so drastic a change in their transfer to the stage that it would almost seem that Shakespeare gleefully composed his romance just to prove the generic inferiority of novels, as his choice of title would seem to indicate.[1] In any case, I shall attempt to show how a purely fictional, as distinct from historical, legendary, or mythical, point of departure allowed him to exploit to their fullest the potentialities of the stage. In other words, his successful struggle with a novel may have enabled him to gain even greater awareness than before of the arcana of his chosen medium.

The Gap in Time

A gap in time, however protracted, causes few problems for writers of fiction, as Charles Perrault's "Sleeping Beauty" and H. G. Wells's *When the Sleeper Wakes* so clearly demonstrate; but it certainly can spell trouble for dramatists, forced by this hiatus to juxtapose two different series of events involving many of the same characters. Indeed, such a gap could produce the divisive effect of an obtrusive tree occupying the foreground of a family photograph. While omniscient novelists seem to thrive on separations in space, dramatists prefer to keep their characters within easy if perilous reach of each other. In bringing *Pandosto* to the stage, Shakespeare had to overcome two formidable obstacles in the guise of spatial and chronological gaps, capable of discouraging even the most skillful playwrights. Indeed, in *The Tempest* he will go to the opposite extreme and, against his usual practice, observe the unities of time, place, and action.[2]

Shakespeare conquered Time by incorporating him (or it) as an ever so slightly ridiculous Chorus into his own production. He thus personified a sixteen-year gap instead of leaving it in glaring abeyance. In any case, the dramatist recasts Time in order to use it as a means of displacement. As Fitzroy Pyle states, "besides stifling critical objections, Time is there simply to pass smoothly ('slide') from one side of the gap to the other."[3] In addition to Time, the Chorus ambiguously represents the author together with his play; and Shakespeare the actor may even have performed the part, thus providing additional justification for the Chorus's lame excuses:

> Impute it not a crime
> To me or my swift passage that I slide
> O'er sixteen years and leave the growth untried
> Of that wide gap, since it is in my power
> To o'erthrow law and in one self-born hour
> To plant and o'erwhelm custom.
>
> (IV.i.4–9)

The Chorus presents the audience not only with an excuse but also with a suitable theory of the theater, particularly in the use of "gap," which, in referring to the sixteen-year hiatus, points to one of the inevitable shortcomings of dramatic representation, since theater can never approximate, let alone coincide with, what it purports to imitate. Indeed, it succeeds only in fully representing itself; and perhaps for this reason, the play in the name of Time boldly designates itself as a gap—as a separation: a dominant metaphor and theme throughout the romance. Moreover, critics have pondered the meaning of "untried;" and Kittredge aptly defines it as: "untouched in presentation."[4] This lack of presentation as well as a deliberate paucity of narrative would seem to indicate an intended "failure" on the part of the play, condemned to remain unfulfilled in its attempt to approximate its other. The gap may thus express far more than a separation in time, for it appears to expose the inherent failure of mimesis. In requesting the audience not to impute to the gap a crime, Time appears to hint that the stage need not always abide by mimesis and referentiality, a suggestion that he confirms in boldly asserting the idea of autonomy, either his own or that of theater, including *The Winter's Tale* itself, which owes so much of its impact to the overthrow of law and the overwhelming of custom. Finally, "the one self-born hour," can refer to theatrical time—self-generated and self-generating—as opposed to the sixteen-year interval, henceforth relegated to fiction.

In expressing an aesthetic viewpoint, Time has frequent recourse to legal terminology. Such words as "error," "crime," "untried," "power," "law," "custom," and, later in his monologue, "order," "received," and "witness" could readily fit into a trial scene. While putting his own play on trial, with the audience serving in the triple capacity of judge, jury, and plaintiff, the author subtly recapitulates Hermione's condemnation by the king her husband together with her subsequent public trial and final acquittal. By means of this essentially verbal device, a theoretical *mise en abyme* of all theater somehow coincides with a symbolic representation of *The Winter's Tale*. But Time does even more than remind the audience of events previously performed before their very eyes, for by resorting to legal terminology he imposes a semblance of order—akin no doubt to the law and custom he has the power to "o'erwhelm." Whatever his destination, Time invariably discovers order: "Let me pass / The same I am, ere ancient'st order was / Or what is now received" (IV.i.9–11), always bearing witness, even to "the freshest things now reigning" (13), which coincide no doubt with natural order. Paradoxically, this order, however natural and compelling it may appear, never wanders far afield from theatrical order, for Time switches from the lexicon of legality to that of the stage: "Your patience this allowing / I turn my glass and give my scene such growing / As you had slept between" (IV.i.15–17). In addressing an audience that he aims to please, he pointedly makes use of a theatrical term, "scene," and indeed presents the events that will immediately follow as "th' argument of Time" (IV.i.29). A symbolic reduction of all stage productions, his hourglass, a container or dispenser of time, functions by means of frequent repetitions and reversals. In its very construction and shape, the hourglass seems to repeat the structure of the play. The separation into symmetrical halves, the exiguous aperture joining the two so as to necessitate periodic reversals reproduce to some extent the relationship between the two parts of the romance, connected one to the other by the narrowest of openings: Perdita's unlikely survival. Actually, the sixteen-year interval that the Chorus so bravely impersonates merely brings to a climax the far less gaping separations that occur throughout the romance. In short, metaphor materializes as Chorus—as a full-fledged, performable role requiring the mediation of an actor.

The Gap in Performance

Time may have successfully bridged the lengthiest hiatus in the play, but it takes less obvious theatrical devices to span the various gaps that appear throughout, notably in the opening dialogue, characterized by unconscious irony.⁵ Camillo in stressing the inseparability of the two princes—"They were trained together in their childhoods, and there rooted betwixt them such an affection which cannot choose but branch now" (I.i.21–23)—borrows his metaphors from nature, a dominant force and actant in the work. Conversely, in describing their kingly behavior since their separation, he switches to the terminology of exchange and fittingly introduces rhetorical devices such as paradox, oxymoron, and chiasmus, all three propitious to the implementation and maintenance of gaps: "their encounters, though not personal, have been royally attorneyed with interchange of gifts, letters, loving embassies; that they have seemed to be together, though absent; shook hands, as over a vast; and embraced, as it were, from the ends of opposed winds" (I.i.25–29). Despite Camillo's optimistic view, such exchange and rhetoric can only increase the distance between the two monarchs, for they systematically replace the intimacy of a direct personal relationship with diplomatic make-believe. Lapsing from the state of nature, they have descended into the modern world of substitution and representation where each king has to assume his assigned part and where innocent games must give way to mature entertainment, including the present play.⁶

Polixenes, who by actually repeating the word stresses the "innocence" of their fun, lapses into the conditional mode, indicative of impossibility:

> Had we pursued that life,
> And our weak spirits ne'er been higher reared
> With stronger blood, we should have answered heaven

Boldly "Not guilty," the imposition cleared
Hereditary ours.
    (I.ii 70–74)

According to Polixenes' unorthodox and hence perilous denial of
original sin, the two friends would have escaped the most insuperable of all gaps: the Fall of man—the Fall from innocence and grace.[7]
And in a sense, this initial cleavage, perhaps because of the king of
Bohemia's show of reluctance in accepting it, provides metaphorically a performative space for the entire romance. We can perhaps view Leontes' stubborn belief in Polixenes' and Hermione's
guilt as repayment for, and the reversal of, unprecedented bliss,
standing in relation to time-bound existence in much the same way
as theater relates to the everyday world. We may even regard the
king's prolonged fit of jealousy as Time's revenge. Hermione playfully interprets Polixenes' assertion of his and his friend's premarital
state of innocence as an accusation: "Grace to boot! / Of this make
no conclusion, lest you say / Your queen and I are devils" (I.ii.80–82).
Her retort, apparently satirizing traditional male attitudes concerning woman's alleged role in the Fall, foreshadows and indeed paves
the way for her husband's accusations against her. Moreover, the
subsequent materialization of Time as performance may also serve
to reverse an imagined state of innocence, tantamount to a denial of
time. By juxtaposing Camillo's and Polixenes' assertions we can surmise that mankind must remain at a distance from both nature and
innocence, neither of which can survive very long on the stage or, for
that matter, in discourse.

By casting himself, for better or for worse, in the part of cuckold,
and expressing Hermione's imagined misconduct in terms of spectacle, Leontes by reason of his paradoxical theatricality isolates himself from the rest of the cast and the offstage audience. He has indeed
opened within himself a performative gap wherein he compulsively
stages a dismaying drama, beginning with an eleven-line aside and
appropriately capped by a theatrical metaphor: "O, that is entertainment / My bosom likes not, nor my brows" (I.ii.118–19). And all the
while, the king vehemently insists on the veracity of representations
or fictions detrimental to his image; and his destructive scenario,

functioning as causal agent, reduces him to instrumental passivity, so much so that Paulina can equate him with his "tyrannous passion" (II.iii.28). A slave to passions, he can no longer function as a successful dramatist and director in spite of his repeated efforts. His courtiers refuse to accept the plot he insists on imposing; and one of them, Paulina, becomes outspokenly rebellious. Although as king he enjoys the prerogative of charting the future, he obviously lacks the right as well as the capacity to modify the past, for instance, in casting without proof his wife in the role of adulteress. He sarcastically tries to foist his version of the events on his nobles by actually coaching and directing them:

> You, my lords,
> Look on her, mark her well. Be but about
> To say "She is a goodly lady," and
> The justice of your hearts will thereto add
> " 'T'is pity she's not honest—honorable."
> (II.i.64–68)[8]

In his attempt to expose his queen, he forces his own words down the throats of the lords, who steadfastly refrain from behaving like acquiescent spectators and puppets. Strange as this may seem, Leontes, even when he behaves like a tyrant, cannot find a single sycophant in the entire cast, whereas Hermione enjoys throughout the outspoken support of the courtiers.[9] Leontes' accusations often express the idea of a gap in time, for instance: "When you have said she's goodly, come between, / Ere you can say she's honest" (II.i.75–76). Since the cleavage originates in the mind of Leontes and stems from his compulsive plot and his universal mistrust, but not from events witnessed by any of his subjects, it reveals a displacement on his part which he does his utmost to impose on others.[10] Indeed, he does not live in the same world as his people and functions, as do most alienated protagonists, in suspended time—a time at variance with the chronological unfolding of events—in which he can interpolate at will his ghastly visions.

The gap supposedly originating in the mind of Leontes actually has strong affinities with the rhetoric of paradox. Not only does he regard himself as "accursed / In being so blest!" (II.i.38–39), but he claims, "There is a plot against my life, my crown, / All's true that is mistrusted" (II.i.47–48). The king's sweeping paradox, which may owe something to the topos of contradiction as well as to the technique of permutation, enables him to assert the "truth" of his most monstrous suspicions. A subjective feeling of mistrust, seemingly confirmed by the flight of Polixenes, will henceforth provide the sole measure and criterion of "truth." By systematically applying the trope of paradox, he manages to turn the world upside down: the queen's celebrated innocence points by reversal to her guilt in the same way that Polixenes' unstinting friendship must degenerate into betrayal. And this rhetorical permutation, in assuring a victorious usurpation by poisonous fiction, enables him to dismiss all contrary opinions, even the oracle of Delphos. Obviously, Leontes, an even more probing novelist than the author of *Pandosto,* can hardly succeed as dramatist. To Leontes alias Pandosto we owe the sixteen-year abeyance, in both the modern and the Elizabethan sense (abomination), that the Chorus so boldly impersonates in substituting theater for fiction. The stage alone can correct the aberrations or approximations of the originating novel, henceforth reduced to the status of intertextual nuisance. Leontes the novelist retains nevertheless two salient aspects of theatricality: the awareness of playing a part and an addiction to spectacle, for not only does he elaborate his fictions but he visualizes them while compelling others to share his visions. He thus combines the functions of novelist, visionary, and failed critic in compulsively providing hallucinatory and voyeuristic misinterpretations of the events in Shakespeare's play as soon as they unfold. In the very act of introducing rifts, he paradoxically reduces distance, taken in the theatrical sense, for his fictional narratives possess, through the intensity of his stage presence, an overpowering sense of immediacy. Thanks to the gap, the scenes of jealousy derive their potent theatricality from the fugal interplay of distance and proximity, for the audience enjoys what we might call, for lack of a more suitable term, a stereoptic view of the proceedings, capable of compensating for any deficiency in narrative.

In addition to its relationship with rhetoric, an instrument of power, the gap has affinities with hierarchy, indicative of separation; and both of them stand at a considerable remove from innocence.

Leontes shows a misplaced respect for language in the very act of accusing the queen:

> O thou thing!
> Which I'll not call a creature of thy place,
> Lest barbarism, making me the precedent,
> Should a like language use to all degrees
> And mannerly distinguishment leave out
> Betwixt the prince and beggar.
> (II.i.82–87)

It would appear, however, that of the kingly prerogatives setting him far above his subjects, Leontes retains mainly those pertaining to the absolutism of language. He insists on remaining verbally a monarch while losing the respect of his subjects, notably of the irrepressible Paulina. When he publicly calls his wife an adulteress, the nobles hyperbolically express their disagreement. One courtier asserts, "I dare my life lay down" (II.ii.130), and Antigonus adds to hyperbole the topos of the world turned upside down, "I'll keep my stables / where I lodge my wife" (134–35), before promising to geld his three daughters if the king should prove the veracity of his allegations. Indeed, rhetoric and elevated language, even in invective, dominate throughout the first part of the romance, characterized by a strong sense of hierarchy. One might even claim that generic differences oppose the first section to the second, as though to translate into theatrical terms and thus reduce the chronological cleavage between them. In the first part, featuring Leontes' overwhelming jealousy and a catastrophic outcome, the author hardly ever deviates from tragedy, while in the second, marked by Autolycus's antics, he rarely swerves from comedy. The violent demise of Antigonus, rich in gallows humor, and the doddering performance of Father Time provide a transition from one genre to another. Only the havoc produced by Paulina's tempestuous outbursts brings a semblance of levity to the initial section. She even gives herself stage directions in preparation for these performances: "If I prove honey-mouthed, let my tongue blister, / And never to my red-looked anger be / The trumpet any more" (II.ii.33–35). Paulina, following perhaps the king's example, creates an initial gap within herself. She separates tongue from anger, instrument

from feeling, language from referent. Moreover, the time difference
between resolution and action, by imperiling her purpose, leads her
to formulate antithetical metaphors as a sort of rehearsal. She may
even have foreseen the failure of her essentially verbal mission: "The
silence often of pure innocence / Persuades when speaking fails"
(II.ii.41–42). But the spectacle of Hermione's prematurely delivered
child—as though the romance did not feature a sufficient number of
time gaps—will inevitably produce an adverse effect on Leontes, sat-
urated with his own visions and rhetoric. Completely immersed in
his own scenario, the king has become immune to the most vehement
protests, weakened in advance by built-in separations and cleavages.

Paulina adds to the various gaps one of her own invention, based
on legalistic metaphors:

> This child was prisoner to the womb and is
> By law and process of great nature thence
> Freed and enfranchised, not a party to
> The anger of the king, nor guilty of,
> If any be, the trespass of the queen.
>
> (II.ii.59–63)

Actually, this statement, however persuasive it may appear, introduces by means of a terminology quite foreign to the "process of
great nature" an additional cleavage between the child and both her
parents, thus foreshadowing Perdita's impending separation and
loss. It will take the transgressions of Florizel and Autolycus to re-
store a "natural" or rather a more pleasurable order, an order no
longer based on a system of exchange, whether in the guise of commerce or repentance. Since justice and injustice, no less foreign to
natural order than diplomatic exchanges, belong in the same camp,
the queen's trial, despite its favorable outcome, merely compounds
the disaster. Justice as such serves only to ratify separation.

Leontes had knowingly pursued revenge to the detriment of his
own image by casting himself in the role of a cuckold betrayed by his
best friend. But the unfolding of his scenario finally results in a spectacle far more shameful in the eyes of his subjects, because his behavior strikes them as childish and tyrannical. After discovering his error, he humbly accepts Paulina's pitiless verdict: "Go on, go on /

Thou canst not speak too much. / I have deserved / All tongues to talk their bitt'rst" (III.ii.213–15). He even insists on perpetuating the definitive spectacle of his evil deeds: "One grave shall be for both. Upon them shall / The causes of their death appear, unto / Our shame perpetual" (III.i.234–36). Always an author even in defeat, he insists on having the tombs of his wife and his son emblazoned with a text perpetuating his injustice. Previously, he had sought to textualize his marital shame by means of a public trial featuring his queen in the role of ill-starred protagonist. Leontes has in this manner enshrined a performative failure as dismal as, but far less noble, than that of Oedipus, victim of a cleavage not of his own making but inflicted by the gods.

Narrowing the Gap

The gallows humor attendant upon the death of Antigonus and the performative clumsiness of Father Time mark, as I have already suggested, the double transition from the first to the second part. More important still, these transitional scenes point to generic struggles pitting fiction against theater, tragedy against comedy. As one might expect, comedy quickly gains the upper hand so as to assure the definitive triumph of theater. The second half of the romance unfolds on a far lower level than the first from both a social and a stylistic point of view. In the fourth and fifth acts, prose passages outnumber scenes in verse, and elevated speech becomes less prevalent even in poetic tirades. From a hierarchical standpoint, the various characters, partaking in a descending movement, tend to assume roles below their social station. Indeed, in the opening scene of the second section, King Polixenes and Lord Camillo disguise themselves as ordinary folk who may pass unnoticed at a sheepshearing feast. Conversely, the Old Shepherd and Clown, thanks to Perdita's treasure, have risen in the world—"grown into an unspeakable estate" (IV.ii.39)—though well below the level of Polixenes' unostentatious court. In the opening scene of the romance, Archidamus had contrasted the magnificence of Sicilia with the modesty of his own land, thus programming one of the salient differences between the two parts. Archidamus, however, did not realize that entertainment can dispense with splendor and that comedy may have a far stronger appeal than pageantry.

The descent to a lower order of behavior consonant with comedy has, however, a more important function than to provide relief from the grimness of the first three acts, for it leads to the reduction if not the abolishment of hierarchy, one of the prime sources of gaps and discrepancies. The farcical ennobling of the shepherd and his son and the questionable triumphs of Autolycus serve a similar purpose.[11] Through indirection haughty Sicilia becomes a target for satire, since laughter alone can generate the power to redeem ostentatious sins by reducing cleavages. In comparison, Leontes' flamboyant display of grief can serve no useful purpose, combining as it does the perpetuation of a gap with a further ratification of hierarchy, synonymous in this instance with marmoreal inscription. The future belongs to Perdita, who by imbricating and harmonizing the roles of princess, shepherdess, and even goddess transforms through reversal an initial dispossession into plenitude.

It so happens that nearly every scene of the final section reverses an event witnessed earlier in the play. Autolycus the rogue and King Leontes, even though they operate at opposite ends of the social spectrum, have parallel theatrical functions. Both behave like authors eager to foist their dubious fictions on others, the rogue for his immediate benefit and the monarch for his undoing. Each of these incompatible characters insists on tarnishing his own image, the king by stamping himself as a cuckold, the scamp by accusing a certain Autolycus of having robbed, beaten, and dressed him in rags. In his self-indictment, Autolycus provides an unflattering résumé of his checkered past, less to gull Clown by denying his well-established identity and playing the part of victim, than to present the audience with a spectacular portrait of himself consonant with his present performance on stage. Moreover, Autolycus's questionable employments as thief and shady peddler provide an ironic commentary on those stately diplomatic exchanges—including Hermione's entreaty to Polixenes—that had replaced the two kings' innocent games and destroyed the immediacy of their relationship. Unfortunately, exchanges, indispensable no doubt to civilized society, generate gaps through substitution and enable a system of traces to masquerade as human existence. Autolycus's con games on the contrary have the advantage of undercutting by performative display all acceptable forms of exchange, synonymous in this particular play with evil—with the Fall. Shakespeare has paradoxically entrusted a scoundrel, who repeatedly designates himself as such, with a mission better suited to a virtuous and disinterested character. True, Autolycus owes his redemptive powers much less to villainy as such than to performative genius. Redemption results indeed from his theatrical prowess, since he shows far greater mastery of the stage than does Leontes and multiplies successful shows instead of repeatedly externalizing the same self-defeating obsession.

In taking the blame while denying his identity, Autolycus follows Leontes' lead by opening up a cleavage while engineering a reversal. This complex operation, far from taking place within himself, serves the overt and practical purpose of fooling a clown while theatrically reiterating on a farcical level Leontes' debasement of his own image. By deliberately separating identity from act, he fabricates a false gap, because, unlike his gulls, the offstage audience immediately identifies Autolycus with his purported victim. His clever scenario, so typical of farce, constructively contributes to the unfolding of the plot and the fostering of dramatic illusion while deconstructing key events of the past. Unlike Leontes, this picaresque character does not take any of his ad hoc identities seriously but appears to consider each one a part he intends to perform to his greatest advantage. He definitely enjoys the superiority of a true professional. Moreover, the mercurial Autolycus can never stand still but must cast himself in, or adapt to, whatever new role the situation and the audience on stage happen to demand. Nor can the other characters ever recognize him, since their total engrossment with the show prevents them from suspecting the performer.

Autolycus, while concealing his identity, does his utmost to remain throughout true to himself and his questionable profession. In naming his alleged assailant, he behaves in the manner of an artist signing a masterpiece. In any event, he justifiably takes pride in his vocation: "If I make not this cheat bring out another and the shearers prove sheep, let me be unrolled and my name put in the book of virtue" (IV.iii.114–17). He seems to worry that performative failure might lead to a (textual) change in casting and deprive him of the role in which he has always starred. But this farcical fear remains quite rhetorical, for the author has underwritten the rogue's unbelievable success in everything he undertakes. Like many another comic character, he hardly distinguishes between villainy and performance; and, like Molière's Mascarille, he would have every right to inscribe below his image, "Vivat [Autolycus] Fourbum Imperator!"[12] Moreover, his aside clearly expresses the ideas of transformation and reversal, so frequent throughout the play. While stating his determination to live up to his casting, Autolycus thus perpetuates in his own way the (de)constructive schema of the romance; and by his theatrical successes as dramatist, director, and actor, he places himself at the farthest remove from Greene's originating novel. Nevertheless, theatrical success does not prevent him from peddling fiction, notably the incredible tales in the form of ballads he sells to gullible yokels. Dressed as a courtier, he invents blood-curdling tortures to frighten the Old Shepherd and Clown. By his ostentatious self-designation and his "winter tales," he repeats in many respects Leontes' self-deception and visions as well as Perdita's impossible recovery. Thanks mainly to his invention of the rogue, the dramatist has distanced himself from Greene's fictional narrative and given free play to his theatrical skills.

The Pastoral Moment

Shakespeare's greatest innovation may have consisted in creating a plausible collage of different kinds of performative inventiveness: not only tragedy and farcical comedy but pastoral scenes full of music and dancing. The cleavage in space and time has opened up the stage to a wide variety of entertainments. While Leontes stars in the tragic and Autolycus in the farcical scenes, Perdita comes into her own in all things pastoral, where her brilliant performances equal in every respect Autolycus's most inspired efforts. Now, "pastoral" carries with it an air of timelessness and even escapism by eluding involvement with daily experience while remaining immune to the evil determinations of fate.[13] As the events it features must take place in suspended time, it can push make-believe even further than do other forms of dramatic literature. But pastoral in *The Winter's Tale* displays various complexities, probably unique in playwriting. Perdita's suspension in time results from and coincides with her suspension between two fathers: the king and the Old Shepherd, riveted by his namelessness to a purely pastoral identity. His unnamed son has found a permanent niche, not within a fold but on stage, where he never fails to live up to his designation as Clown. This leaves only Perdita, a "real" shepherdess able to function to perfection in timeless pastoral. Far from competing with her, her sheep-shearing companions remain ignorant yokels ready to succumb to the wiles of Autolycus.

Perdita, displaced from and ignorant of her identity as princess, behaves as though she had never strayed very far from a palace. As she could hardly have acquired aristocratic manners in a shepherd's household, her behavior defies verisimilitude while remaining theatrically necessary and therefore convincing within the general frame of romance. Suspended between two identities, two families, two kingdoms, and dreading the gap in rank separating her from the prince, she suffers from a cleavage programmed by her name; but she possesses the ability to bridge it by performative endeavors. She indeed adds the performative trace of Hermione, whom she physically resembles, to her present casting as humble shepherdess. Her theatrical movement toward recuperation helps to compensate for her father's descent into the abyss. Ironically, Leontes' sixteen years of repentance and his fictional bent do not exclude theatricality. Cleomenes summarizes them in terms of spectacle and exchange:

Sir, you have done enough, and have performed
A saint-like sorrow. No fault could you make
Which you have not redeemed—indeed paid down
More penitence than done trespass.
                              (V.i.1–4)

To performative displacement Perdita adds a movement in time as though to minimize her sixteen-year severance from origins. Through verbal and floral manipulation she tends, as we shall see, to collapse the seasons and, by this device, speed up time as though to catch up with her lost past. In this manner, her name, meaning, according to the oracle,"that which is lost" (III.ii.134), antithetically programs her recovery. Upon their very first appearance on stage, Florizel playfully changes his beloved's name into the metonymic origin of his own: "These your unusual weeds to each part of you / Do give a life—no shepherdess, but Flora / Peering in April's front!" (IV.iv.1–3). As Perdita has dressed not for her usual part of shepherdess, but for a festive occasion, the prince's hyperbole praises her masquerade while expressing the intensity of his passion. An incarnation of Flora, the Roman goddess of flowers and mother of Spring, she presides at a ritual connected with natural cycles. But the role of goddess happens to distance her from her present designation while bringing her closer to her future and past casting as princess. The prince has thus nominally added another suspension, this time a dynamic interim leading ever upward.

In the course of this pastoral interim, Perdita, in keeping with her mythological designation, multiplies floral metaphors, fraught with time gaps, for she bravely attempts to bestow flowers in accordance with age and status. She assigns to the middle-aged Polixenes and Camillo, perhaps disguised as old men, plants capable of outlasting the season, but even less appropriate to their age than such midsummer blossoms as "Hot lavender, mints, savory, marjoram," and especially the personified and passionate "marigold, that goes to bed wi' th' sun / And with him rises weeping" (IV.iv.105–7):

> Reverend sirs,
> For you there's rosemary and rue; these keep
> Seeming and savor all the winter long.
> Grace and remembrance be to you both,
> And welcome to our shearing!
> (IV.iv.72–77)

"Rue," though emblematic of grace, suggests bitterness, characterizing a past she cannot remember together with King Polixenes' hidden resentment, while "rosemary," standing for remembrance, offers more promising connotations. The use of the term "seeming" to designate color subtly introduces the idea of performance, in keeping with the allegorization of flowers. She carefully points out that the sheepshearing festival takes place before summer's end:

                    Sir, the year growing ancient,
Not yet on summer's death nor on the birth
Of trembling winter, the fairest flowers o' th' season
Are our carnations and streaked gillyvors,
Which some call nature's bastards. Of that kind
Our rustic garden's barren, and I care not
To get slips of them.
          (IV.iv.79–85)

Approaching autumn, in awkward abeyance between midsummer
and early winter, remains unnamed, as though it had lost its identity
and could serve no better function than to provide the shortest transition from one period to the next. We may wonder why the heroine
skips over the season of greatest abundance, a season better suited than
any other to the age of her two guests. True, summer and winter, despite
their naming, fare no better than the intervening months, for she shows
the former at the threshold of death and the latter as "trembling," no
doubt from icy decrepitude. By means of a rhetorical reversal, she relates the dying of summer to the birth of winter; and she manages to collapse three of the seasons either by pointing to their demise or curtailing
their existence. All along she plays the part of Flora, emblematic of eter-
nal springtime and rebirth. Faithful to this role, she objects to the arti-
ficiality of "carnations" and "gillyvors," designated as "nature's bastards." Unjustly deemed a bastard by her father, she fittingly rejects
anything that might smack of illegitimacy.

    Her desire to award suitable flowers to her contemporaries, such as
the prince and her companions, generates a rift of a different sort: a discrepancy between appropriateness of assignment and availability. Her
impossible wish expressed in the conditional mode leads to highly lyrical discourse, providing directions for an unperformable scene where
blossoms, as absent as her own past, become through personification
and mythological associations allegories of love, for instance:

                    pale primroses,
That die unmarried, ere they can behold
Bright Phoebus in his strength—a malady
Most incident to maids.
          (IV.iv.122–25)

In the course of her speech, she metamorphoses herself, if not into Flora, at least into a performer playing that part:

> Methinks I play as I have seen them do
> In Whitsun pastorals. Sure this robe of mine
> Does change my disposition.
> (IV.iv.133–35).

Her embarrassed awareness provides more than a simple meta-dramatic interruption, for it distances her even more than before from her immediate surroundings, her humble rank, and her lofty origins. This state of suspension and separation reaches a climax at the moment when she most clearly spells out her love. Nonetheless, her forwardness in this instance may remind us of the directness previously displayed by Hermione in revealing her feelings.[14]

During the festivities, not only Perdita, but the king and Camillo by their disguise, the prince by playing the part of swain, together with all the shepherds and shepherdesses consciously stage performances. But the heroine proves her superiority by upstaging every one of them and eliciting at the very least the grudging applause of the most hostile member of her audience, the king, who appropriately expresses his admiration in terms of a cleavage:

> Nothing she does or seems
> But smacks of something greater than herself,
> Too noble for this place.
> (IV.iv.157–59)

A player could hardly wish for greater praise than Polixenes' prophetic utterance. Florizel, eager to see his fondest wishes fulfilled, euphuistically stresses the nobility of his beloved:

> Each your doing,
> So singular in each particular,
> Crowns what you are doing in the present deeds,
> That all your acts are queens.
> (IV.iv.143–46)

Through her performative deeds as player and dancer, Perdita has attained the highest rank, thus showing that theater, even in maintaining distance, retains the power to join together what fiction has sundered. Theater alone, through the performative prowess of the heroine, can focus, channel, and organize all past and future events in the romance. Perdita in the role of Flora, by placing herself on a different plane, equidistant from that of shepherdess and princess, but combining the qualities of both, spares herself the alienation that, through fiction, had plagued her family. In any case, her star role during the festivities should allay the fears she had expressed after donning her costume:

> O, the Fates!
> How would he look, to see his work, so noble,
> Vilely bound up? What would he say? Or how
> Should I, in these my borrowed flaunts, behold
> The sternness of his presence?
> (IV.iv.20–24)

Henceforth, Perdita, bolstered by the king's applause, need no longer fear his angry countenance or dread the social gap that separates her from the prince: "To me the difference forges dread" (IV.iv.17).

Rhetoric and Exchange

Performance has much in common with rhetoric, perhaps because both of them heighten, but do not necessarily change, an event. If we can believe the servant, Autolycus combines hyperbole with performance in order to sell his wares: "Why, he sings 'em over as they were gods or goddesses" (IV.iv.206–7). Clown had previously admitted to a curiously oxymoronic taste in music: "I love a ballad but even too well if it be doleful matter merrily set down, or a very pleasant thing indeed and sung lamentably" (IV.iv.187–190). Absurd and contradictory though it may seem, this statement sheds light upon the romance as a whole by pointing to discrepancy and ambiguity in performance. Clown has formulated in his inimitable way the aesthetics of displacement, involving distancing of various sorts, including the crucial cleavage between referent and performance. Moreover, he expresses his views in the form of an antithetical chiasmus, a trope that happens to apply to the entire play because of the numerous parallelisms and imbrications by which its two colliding parts fit together.

The ballad concerning a midwife's extraordinary delivery, assuredly one of Autolycus's best sellers, relates to the first part by means of exchange and rhetoric. The midwife by her revealing name, "Taleporter"—one who carries stories and no doubt provides professional help in engendering them—reduces textuality, fiction, and exchange to their lowest and most incredible levels. A "ballad in print" (IV.iv.255), and therefore, according to Mopsa, true, recounts "how a usurer's wife was brought to bed of twenty money-bags at a burthen, and how she longed to eat adders' heads and toads carbonadoed" (258–60). This tall tale, by allowing exaggeration to scale unheard of heights, compounds diabolical exchange and hyperbole. From the standpoint of the audience, the yokels' credulity performatively repeats on a purely farcical level Leontes' obsessive belief in the fictions and distorted perceptions generated by his imagination.[15]

The author tends to present exchange in a bad light throughout the play, but usually without heaping ridicule on it. Polixenes, still disguised, reproaches his son for not buying presents for Perdita, only to leave himself open to a metaphorical retort:

The gifts she looks from me are packed and locked
Up in my heart, which I have given already,
But not delivered
　　(IV.iv.351–53).

Instead of exchanging trinkets for favors, Florizel intends to provide his beloved with the greatest gift of all: his heart, a metonymy for his entire being. In this declaration of love, he makes strong use of hyperbole in connection with his service to Perdita as though to reverse their disproportionate difference in rank.

Florizel reaches rhetorical heights and depths in the use of hyperbole in his address to Camillo:

Not for Bohemia nor the pomp that may
Be thereat gleaned, for all the sun sees or
The close earth wombs or the profound seas hide

In unknown fathoms, will I break my oath
To this my fair beloved.
            (IV.iv.481–85)

Hyperbole in this instance expresses the strength of his love and the
stubbornness of his resolve. Camillo sees the hopelessness of making
the young prince change his mind in much the same way that sixteen
years earlier he had realized that nothing could cure Leontes of his relentless jealousy. The hyperbole of Florizel's positive passion moves
of course in a direction diametrically opposed to that of the destructive obsessions of the king of Sicilia. And Camillo reacts to the
prince's rhetoric by immediately sailing back in his company to his
native land in much the same way he had escaped to Bohemia with
Polixenes. Contrapuntal relations of this sort, which serve to coun-
teract the tragic reversals of the first part of the play, properly belong
to romance, for such hidden exchanges between tragic and favorable
events differ considerably from the more overt and mechanical permutations typical of comedy. In reacting to the hyperbolic fictions of
the "rhetorically flamboyant" Leontes and the amorous eloquence of
Florizel, Camillo on the spur of the moment turns into a remarkably
successful dramatist and director who invents the plot, places the
cues, and thoroughly coaches his players.[16] Impelled to a certain extent by ostentatious rhetoric quite foreign to his role and function,
Camillo engineers dramaturgic switches from tragic obsession and
pastoral lyricism to suspenseful drama. His two departures differ
from one another in the way an anguished decision might deviate
from clever scheming, or tragic from comic peripeteia. His sudden
return to Sicilia eliminates in addition a spatial separation and exile—his own as well as Perdita's—equivalent to a sixteen-year gap in
time.

Art as Cleavage

Hermione's return to life, by all odds the most dramatic scene in the
romance and the one marking the clearest departure from Greene's
novel, has justifiably generated a considerable number of perceptive
commentaries dealing with the profound meaning of the play. I shall

bracket once again undeniable depths and address only the theatrical aspects of this unique scene so as to show how the author followed in the footsteps of Pygmalion, a far more mimetically successsful artist than even Julio Romano. Shakespeare had to bring art to life, a task somewhat easier than that of Ovid's hero, for the dramatist needed only to disguise an actor as a stage prop or, better still, to switch from one level of representation to another. Switching plays indeed a crucial part in the scene, not only in the change from death to life and from artifact to performance, but from immobility to movement.

From a purely theatrical standpoint, the progression from immobility to mobility or from stasis to dynamism consists in exchanging or substituting one mode of artistic representation for another. Hermione's progression from statue to character repeats, moreover, the movement of the play from winter—a winter of discontent—to spring and rebirth, providing in this respect a final *mise en abyme* of the entire romance.[17] The discovery that the queen, dead and buried these sixteen years, has survived stamps the event as just another "winter's tale," even less credible than Perdita's miraculous preservation, authenticated at least by the novelist. As we see this story enacted before our eyes, we cannot help but endow it with performative truth. After all, Hermione, whether we consider her a work of art or a character, remains at a safe distance from the audience as well as from daily existence, so Shakespeare's best efforts have produced no more and no less than a concluding generic metamorphosis even more radical than the constant substitution of theater for fiction. Since we may regard a statue as a representation even further removed from stage productions than a novel, its transformation into a live performance brings to a brilliant climax a concatenation of theatrical maneuvers while providing an acceptable denouement for the plot.

However opposed to one another they may appear, sculptures and theatrical representations have one important feature in common: mimesis, for both of them purport to imitate life. At the unveiling the king, reduced to silent wonderment, praises the true-to-life representation of the queen: "Her natural posture! / Chide me, dear stone, that I may say indeed / Thou art Hermione" (V.iii.23–35). His appreciation conforms no doubt to contemporary theory concerning the powerful effect of imitation in art, a theory against which Fawnia, Perdita's model, had cautioned her audience: "Painted eagles are pictures, not eagles. Zeuxis' grapes were like grapes, yet shadows."[18] More important still, Leontes and his daughter show empathy with the ambiguous sculpture even to the extent of imitating its behavior. The magic of the "royal piece" (V.iii.38), according to the king, "From thy admiring daughter took the spirits, / Standing like stone with thee" (V.iii.41–42). While Perdita adopts the posture of a statue, her father pays close attention to the queen's actual appearance, for he notices that the artist has represented her not in youth but in middle age, thus abolishing one of the gaps or barriers separating them. Leontes simultaneously experiences the frigidity of sculpture: "Does not the stone rebuke me / For being more stone than it?" (V.iii.37–38). Moreover, by addressing the statue he transforms it into a member of the cast, a device that helps to smooth the transition from stage prop to dramatis persona. His perplexed awareness of Hermione's wrinkles does not prevent him from moving back in time:

> O, thus she stood,
> Even with such life of majesty—warm life,
> As now it coldly stands—when first I wooed her!
> (V.iii.34–36).

Despite or perhaps by reason of his faults, Leontes maintains a strong sense of continuity:

> My lord, your sorrow was too sore laid on,
> Which sixteen winters cannot blow away,
> So many summers dry. Scarce any joy
> Did ever so long live; no sorrow
> But killed itself much sooner.
> (V.iii.49–53)

By personifying sorrow, Camillo points once again to the king's weakness in the face of intense emotion. Only Hermione's stubbornness in remaining alive can match the passive persistence of her husband.

In addressing the king, Paulina speaks in terms of a spectator's reaction to performance:

If I had thought the sight of my poor image
Would thus have wrought you—for the stone is mine—
I'ld not have showed it"
        (V.iii.57–59).

By her use of "wrought," Paulina underscores the close relationship
between image and viewer. The king's emotion not only results from,
but coincides with, Julio Romano's supposed workmanship. But all
along the audience keenly realizes that, however "wrought," Leontes
and Hermione engage, actively as well as passively, in performing
their assigned parts. Indeed, the more the characters heap praise on
the statue, the more they increase the theatricality of the situation by
gradually moving from perception to participation, from distance to
immediacy. Paulina has to warn Leontes and Perdita not to embrace
or even touch the freshly painted statue gradually coming to life.
When Paulina proposes to draw the curtain and put an end to the spectacle, Leontes objects: "No, not these twenty years" (V.iii.84); and his
daughter adds, "So long could I / Stand by, a looker on" (84–85). As this
time span would exceed sixteen years of exile and sorrow, father and
daughter, whose attendance at the show must coincide with life itself,
stand out as among the most receptive and active spectators in the history of the stage. Sight for them must obviously coincide with participation. Paulina's fear that contemplation of the statue might drive Leontes
mad points once again to analogies between the two parts of the romance. But the king would welcome twenty years of such insanity: "No
settled senses of the world can match / The pleasure of that madness"
(V.iii.72–73). Ironically, both his somber and his pleasurable madness
result from visions, the first, as he himself acknowledges, a fiction of his
imagination, the second a seemingly miraculous representation by a famous if anachronistic Italian artist.

Leontes' appreciation of the statue comes to a climax at the very
moment he reaches the brink, so to speak, of participation:

                    Still methinks
There is an air comes from her. What fine chisel
Could ever yet cut breath? Let no man mock me,
For I will kiss her.
        (V.iii.77–80)

Total engrossment, by eliminating the gap between spectator and spectacle, not only would lead to participation, but might spoil the show, Shakespeare's no less than Paulina's. Indeed, the king's and Perdita's eagerness, brought to their highest pitch thanks to Paulina's masterly staging, gives the necessary signal and cue for the performance to proceed. To the sound of music, Hermione makes her spectacular descent from the pedestal. As Frey so aptly puts it, "When the stillness breaks, references to time flood forth."[19] Nonetheless, time though unnamed had all along made its presence felt, even when Hermione played the part of statue. Theater indeed cannot succeed unless it provides a sense of time through performance. And theater, in the final scene, has reconciled art with fiction by forcing them both to perform side by side in accordance with dramatic timing. Willy-nilly, they have become members, if not necessarily the stars, of the cast. Their performance, consisting at least in part of the metamorphosis of an artistic stage prop into a living player, bridges the widest gap in the play, a gap that transcends the sixteen year interval between the two sections, for Hermione, unlike her counterpart in *Pandosto*, has unexpectedly returned from the world of the dead. For this reason, art in the semblance of a masterpiece by Julio Romano has had to come to the aid of performance, which had easily sufficed to bridge ordinary gaps: those that take place in time. The triumph over death demands a more drastic kind of theatrical representation: a cold and motionless monument that lovingly rejoins the cast.[20]

EIGHT

The Interplay of Aesthetics
and Theatricality

Although concluding remarks usually succeed in tying a few loose ends together, more often than not they provide an aftermath or, better still, an armistice, clearing the deck for further textual skirmishes. Rodrigue's imperishable words in Corneille's *Le Cid,* "Le combat cessa faute de combattants" (The combat ceased for lack of combatants [IV.iii.1328]), might thus serve as an epigraph to the final chapter of many a critical study, triumphant or not, for at the end of the play the hero, for the sake of love, challenges all comers. It would seem therefore that conclusions tend to look toward future developments while giving a semblance of direction to past accomplishments. As the present book might reasonably serve as a preamble for an aesthetic study of theatricality, my concluding remarks, in addition to pointing out connections among the various chapters, will address, but without anticipating a definitive solution, a crucial issue involving playwriting, critical theory, and above all the aesthetics of performance.

Ever since Coleridge and until quite recently, critics concerned with exploring the mimetic or referential aspects of Shakespeare's theater have insisted on praising him for the depth of his insights as moralist, psychologist, and political scientist—in short, for his unparalleled understanding of human nature or, in more existential terms, of the human condition, movingly expressed by so many of his characters more often in despair than in triumph. At the same time, these critics have realized that no dramatist before or since has shown greater mastery of, and a more radical commitment to, the stage. The same paradox obviously applies in varying degrees to other major playwrights, particularly to those who, like Shakespeare, actively participated in the production of their works, for instance Sophocles, Molière, Ibsen, Brecht, Ionesco. Scholars for this reason have found themselves in the same sort of impasse as King Laios's ghost in Cocteau's *Infernal Machine*. Brave Laios vanishes each time he attempts to voice his forbidden message and lapses into silence whenever he seeks to manifest a visible presence; similarly, scholars tend to lose touch with the stage in the very act of pursuing content and to ignore deep meanings whenever they focus too narrowly on theatrical technique. Thus, while all characters suffer from one kind or another of performative failure, though usually in a less frustrating manner than the perplexed Theban king, exegetes eagerly and in great numbers condone in the name of scholarship their willful failures as audience.

The device of emphasizing metatheater and entertainment by no means guarantees that a critic will not fail as audience, particularly if he refrains from taking advantage of celebrated stagings but tries instead to derive metaphoric clues for performance from close and, hence, poetic readings of the script. He can never resist the temptation of substituting for the play itself a more or less performative metalanguage derived in part from the original piece and in part from his own inventiveness. In any case, this critic has placed the burden of interpretation on a limited number of metaphors and tropes at the expense of other keys the overdeterminations of which would have yielded different but equally viable metalanguages. But didn't Wallace Stevens evoke twenty-four separate ways of looking at a reciprocating blackbird, arguably a less spectacular creature, even for stagestruck birdwatchers, than any of the six plays discussed?

The theatrical approach followed in these pages has undoubtedly and even deliberately failed to provide any new or useful general information about Shakespeare and his times. Although some of my comments may here and there suggest an interpretation that perchance has escaped the notice of specialists, my chief purpose, as I have already stated, has consisted all along in exploring, in the light of Shakespeare's practice, some of the metaphorical operations involved in composing performable scripts. I have, moreover, emphasized uniqueness and difference rather than universality by treating each play as a sui generis but nonetheless exemplary dramatic construct. Such an endeavor will hardly surprise followers of Paul Valéry, who regarded every major work of art not only as unique and as a law unto itself but as deserving the respect usually shown to thoroughly elaborated, self-sufficient metaphysical constructs, and therefore no less capable than conceptual systems of generating, among other metadiscourses, their own aesthetic schemes. Conversely, he treated major metaphysicians as artistic geniuses who in their unrelenting pursuit of the absolute elaborated no more and no less than exquisite and self-sufficient artifacts only incidentally involving truth.[1]

My performative readings of the six plays would indeed suggest that each masterpiece succeeds in fostering its own system of dramatic values and, hence, its own particular and unrepeatable aesthetic system as well as its own theory of theatricality. *Much Ado about Nothing* thoroughly explores and develops the potentialities of permutation, as though a choreographer had arrogated the prerogatives of a dramatist or as if a playwright had invaded the territory of a choreographer. The entire comedy suggests a gigantic *comparaison rapportée,* or interchange based on false attribution, in which the plot and the performers repeatedly exchange twists and turns with the peripeteia of country dancing. The play's unfolding would seem to suggest that the author has endeavored to explore and exploit in terms of spectacle an imaginary and marginal space where drama, music, and dance would finally merge. Marginality by no means implies superficiality, but suggests rather a dynamic system of exchange: the proper semantic domain, in my opinion, of aesthetics, which thrives less on (referential) being than on tangents, substitutions, displacements, shifts, and denials, invariably at the expense of day-to-day existence or historical reconstruction. The comedy would appear to owe its aesthetic success to the systematic undermining of psychological continuity, moral consistency, and motivation, gradually replaced by performative gestures such as terpsichorean and rhetorical permutations. Superficiality turns the tables on profundity; and the medium completely eclipses the message, as the title of the play would seem to promise.

Twelfth Night poses an aesthetic problem as unique and as worthy of exploration as permutation. A festive interplay of interlocking frames and permeations dominates the comedy no less in plot and characterization than in language. Analogy, by indicating the interpenetration of opposing forces through metaphorical manipulation, assumes for this reason an even more crucial function than in *Much Ado about Nothing*, a comedy that features from beginning to end a series of interacting and imbricated figures of speech. As provider of substitute motives and as shaper of imaginary performative spaces, this rhetorical system operates as a sort of marginalized but effective dramatist, thriving on misdirection. While the frames in *Twelfth Night* do not possess such occult powers, for their manipulation involves mainly though not exclusively the scene, they reveal nonetheless from a quite different perspective some of the key operations of theater. The emphasis on framing actually transforms the visible scene into a dynamic metaphorical space geared to entrap the unwary and deny permanence or even consistency to characterization and motivation. Framing thus possesses some of the disruptive power provided by rhetoric in *Much Ado about Nothing*: both of them somehow serve the purpose of performance by shifting and finally neutralizing the impact of reality. Once again such seemingly superficial and tangential elements as framing and unframing, in this instance directly connected with the machinery of stage production rather than with performances only indirectly associated with drama, function as the determining factors. In keeping with the title, carnival carries the day or rather the night.

Framing remains the determining factor in *Measure for Measure*, a play marked by oppositions and permeations as well as by a gigantic permutation between eroticism and death, paradoxically having only parody and irony in common with a traditional *danse macabre*. Nonetheless, this comedy by no means repeats the interactions characteristic of the two previous works, because of the presence throughout of a powerful surrogate dramatist who maneuvers the other players with the mastery of a disguised puppeteer. Even though he pulls all the strings, he maintains a threatened and, hence, persuasively theatrical presence thanks to Lucio's contesting voice and to the contrived absurdity of the newly enforced "old" law, which perversely reduces the credibility of the plot.[2] In any event, the author managed to solve the difficult theatrical problem of transforming a godlike and dominant protagonist into a viable performer, quite incapable of ever leaving the stage for some transcendent but problematical world in, or perhaps beyond, the wings. Shakespeare subsequently gave a quite different solution to a similar problem in *The Tempest,* where Prospero regretfully abandons his overwhelming mastery over all things theatrical upon his resumption of political power. Vincentio, however, must remain forever faithful to his theatrical calling, even and perhaps especially when he delegates his prerogatives to an understudy. As in *King Lear,* drama actually thrives on the delegation and substitution of authority. But the Duke shows a clear advantage as dramatist over the unfortunate king, for he only feigns to relinquish his power. His false exit actually leads to a multiplication of performative spaces, each one generating its own tentative scenarios. Angelo all by himself sets up two quite different and overlapping plays, the first, centrally located, ostensibly composed in the name of his master, the second, offstage and clandestine, wrought and performed by himself in his own name as fallen angel. And all the while Lucio invents plots pertaining more often than not by reason of their irrelevance to elusion. A wiser person would have left the composing of plays to competent dramatists and never departed from the function of prompter. Framing and unframing make their presence felt throughout the play and function aesthetically in a unique manner by providing stages for an overwhelmingly dominant dramatist, who operates as an extension of the author himself. Thanks to this sidetracking and bracketing of the real profundities of this problem play, a metaphorical puppet show emerges in order to assure the triumph of the stage. All three comedies offer, each in its own particular way, a sort of *schème constructeur,* freely translated as a structuring prehension, resulting in a continual not to say geometrical progression of performative elements.[3] And in each of the three plays theatrical machinery gravitates toward perpetual motion.

While comedies, at least those of Shakespeare, evidence mainly an expansive movement, tragedies, whether or not they expand and dilate, display locking mechanisms that invariably lead to stoppage. They move along grandly toward a definitive gridlock rather than toward perpetual motion. In *Oedipus*, this gridlock waits for the action to unfold before revealing its unshakable permanence. In Racine, fate holds the protagonist and indeed most of the principals in its grip, all the more so because it has found powerful allies in two of the unities, perceived as impositions of time and place, which pervade the metaphorical fabric of the plays. Shakespeare, even in his tragedies, allows himself and his characters far more freedom, and he has little use for the infernal machinations of fate. Neither Othello nor Hamlet nor Lear nor even Macbeth can legitimately place the blame on destiny or the gods. Their catastrophe depends on causes for which they might, in a prologue or epilogue, assume full responsibility, for they invariably arise from their own performative failure or, in the case of Hamlet and even Othello, their perilous performative success. The Moor actually owes his downfall to freedom rather than constraint. The author may have given him too much rope instead of tying him down from the very beginning. And only Shakespeare, who knew how to take full advantage of the freedom of Elizabethan theater, could have thought of reducing the epic to low satire and high adventure to domesticity in order to engineer a generic breakthrough. In spite of its tragic outcome, *Othello* shares several of the characteristics of the three comedies, for instance the rhetorical causality that marks *Much Ado about Nothing*, the separating frames so crucial to both *Twelfth Night* and *Measure for Measure*, and especially the propensity of minor causes to produce disproportionate effects featured in all the plays. Although motivation appears reliable and consistent in *Othello*, it nonetheless depends for its causal effects on a performative quality that the protagonist and his ancient happen to share with the author: the ability to tell persuasive tales. It would seem that fiction, originating in dramatic practice, can rival if not outweigh motivation and the other mimetic factors on which we so frequently rely in explaining the unfolding and outcome of tragedy. In any case, the search for performative clues—the search for the overdeterminations of the medium—yields similar results whether applied to tragedy or to comedy. *Othello* possesses, of course, an abundance of unique theatrical qualities, notably the

schism between casting and stage presence, the protagonist's severance from a field of action worthy of him, the ensuing substitution of
domesticity for heroics, and the perpetual recourse to fiction. The
play depends for its success on systematic and parallel reductions of
an epic universe, whereby one performative mode parasitizes and de-
molishes another. *King Lear,* probably the most harrowing tragedy
ever composed, succeeds in a very different but equally theatrical
manner through the self-induced reduction of the protagonist from
dramatist to actor and finally to spectator, where he pathetically
joins a distraught audience, compelled to function as an echoing
chorus.

Hamlet, in many respects the most modern of Shakespeare's
plays, features, from the standpoint of metatheater, a conflict between a playwright proposing to stage a drama of revenge, and his
protagonist, an actor doubling as critic, in search of a much more sophisticated part than that of avenger. As Hamlet unfortunately does
not possess Vincentio's power to stage scenarios at will and cast himself in the authoritative role he happens to find suitable, but must on
the contrary play a distasteful part in his uncle's unseemly production, he systematically has recourse to elusion, which enables him to
function at least temporarily on the margins rather than at the center
of action, where he plays games of his own invention—for instance
in ever so slightly rearranging a scenario contrived for his own destruction. The success of the play depends to a large degree on the deliberately perverse refusals of the author and of his main character to
live up—or down—to the audience's usual expectations. As we
might expect, *Hamlet* displays an abundance of unique theatrical
features capable of setting or changing the entire course of dramatic
art. For one thing, it already relies on aesthetic conceptions that Pirandello will rediscover three centuries later. So why should we
worry with T. S. Eliot about a missing "objective correlative"
grounded in mimesis if the hero insists on transforming into spectacle a hidden script and putting on shows only marginally related to
his assigned part?[4]

Shakespeare may have composed *The Winter's Tale* as a direct
challenge to the classicists, including of course his rival Ben Jonson.
From just about every point of view, this romance should lead to a

dramatic disaster, for it appears to consist of collages not only of antagonistic genres but of warring plots. Far from attempting to conceal or at least mitigate the differences among its many divisions, it actually flaunts them by designating at every turn, and deliberately falling into, a multiplicity of abysses. But it so happens that by overdetermining separations, particularly the sixteen-year abeyance between the opening and closing sections, the author has transformed gaps into causal agents that, with the help of a subtle system of analogies, explain and harmonize a multiplicity of discrepancies. In addition, the romance features a dazzling array of entertainments, all of them making up for Leontes' protracted and dismal one-man show improvised and performed for the benefit of an audience of captive courtiers. It would seem that romance adheres to the principles of comedy rather than tragedy, for it relies on an expanding performance that precludes gridlock. The play characteristically ends when a statue sets itself in motion and joins a happy throng.

To conclude, I shall make a single attempt at generalization. The six works discussed appear to indicate that the triumph of theatricality in Shakespearean as well as other successful drama depends on the firm control exerted by rhetorical byplay, including of course metaphor, over all forms of verisimilitude and mimesis, whether in plot or in characterization. Moreover, each of the six plays suggests that these rhetorical determinations can assure, by means of substitutions, the dominance of the medium. Because of this prevalence of rhetoric, the attempt to explain the impact of a play as dependent upon the audience's willingness to suspend disbelief appears unsatisfactory and may apply only to minor works. Indeed, practically every major dramatic piece repeats in a variety of ways its designation as theater. But how can theater in the very act of proclaiming itself an illusion—of denying any claim to reality—move an audience? The example of Shakespeare suggests that the reaction of the public, including catharsis, depends far less on a persuasive imitation of "reality," including the customs and conceptions of Shakespeare's contemporaries, than on the manipulative power of the medium.

For this reason, the actual operations and contrivances purportedly leading to mimesis may matter far more than the resulting imitation or representation. Metatheater would thus assume several dis-

tinct but complementary functions. Or rather we can define and interpret it from three quite different perspectives insofar as the term
"metatheater" or "metadrama" may simply refer to discourse concerning stage production embodied in the play, or, in a somewhat
more complex manner, it may indicate that the play in question
overtly or covertly shows awareness of itself as theater, or finally that
the play as medium tends to substitute its own characteristic operations for, and sometimes at the expense of, whatever "reality" it
claims to represent. Throughout the book, I have treated metadrama
mainly as a system of substitutions which serve to displace the referent while pretending to copy it. And these substitutions succeed essentially because the dramatist has abundantly overburdened the
events together with the characters' reactions to them by means of a
variety of performative metaphors. In short, an effective dramatist
systematically translates everything derived from the fable and human experience into the terms best suited to his/her medium. As Kenneth Burke has stated, Shakespeare's characters' "life-like quality,
the illusion of their being fully rounded out as people, really derives
from his dramaturgic skill in finding traits that act well, and in giving
his characters only traits that suit them for the action needed of
them."[5] I might add that Shakespeare specializes in traits that readily
lend themselves to a performative unfolding of the action and that in
so doing he has placed purely theatrical considerations above all
other preoccupations. Drama cannot of course accede to wholeness,
and even a cursory analysis will reveal in any play whatsoever a number of holes or even gaps. Whatever human coherence and consistency the audience so generously attributes to a play or to a character
would thus appear to result from the irresistible performative surge
of the medium rather than from the representation of a fabled reality.
Shakespeare's theater can stand as exemplary insofar as he has, perhaps more than any playwright before or since, let the stage speak for
itself, but without unduly flaunting its self-consciousness in the manner of postmodern drama.

NOTES

1. Metatheater and Performance

1. All Shakespeare quotations come from the Pelican edition of *The Complete Works*.

2. In accordance with the dramatistic maneuvers described by Burke in his *Grammar of Motives*. See also his article "*Othello*: An Essay to Illustrate a Method."

3. See in this connection Pechter, "The New Historicism and Its Discontents."

4. For a justification of deconstruction and, indeed, of close textual reading, see "The Triumph of Theory." Hartman and Parker, in *Shakespeare and the Question of Theory*, provide valuable poststructural studies, more authentically deconstructive but far less theatrically oriented than mine, by Howard Felperin, Robert Weimann, Margaret W. Ferguson, and Terence Hawkes, as well as by the two editors themselves. In *Literary Fat Ladies*, Patricia Parker, by means of a poststructural rhetorical approach, has made an important contribution to Shakespearean studies, particularly in the chapter "Transfigurations: Shakespeare and Rhetoric," pp. 67–96. For a balanced assessment of poststructural contributions to Shakespearean studies, see Robert Weimann's recent article "Shakespeare (De)Canonized."

5. Both difference and analogy make their presence felt in the numerous puns that Jacques Derrida and Philippe Lacoue-Labarthe introduce in so many of their works. Puns rely more often than not on the unstable and often explosive contiguity of likeness and difference. Moreover, the poststructural concept of *écriture* can paradoxically lend itself to personification and may even border on metaphysics by rivaling in its pervasiveness Bergsonian duration. We may of course ask to what extent a play, treated primarily as a per-

formative score, pertains to *écriture*. Of all deconstructive strategies, I have found displacement the most useful in dealing with drama. By "displacement," a term discussed at greater length later in this chapter, I designate a theatrical movement, either within the play itself, or between the text of the dramatic work and the event (or environment) to which it purportedly refers and that it pretends to represent while undermining it.

6. Bergson, *L'Evolution créatrice*, pp. 272–98.

7. Derrida, "La Différance," pp. 41–68. For a discussion of this subject, see Derrida, *Derrida and Différance*.

8. Parker, *Literary Fat Ladies*, p. 9.

9. For metaphor as delay and distance, see ibid., pp. 47ff.

10. Derrida , "La Différance," p. 46.

11. Bergson, *Les Données immédiates* , pp. 105–107.

12. A discrepancy first noted and explained by Cleanth Brooks in *The Well-Wrought Urn*.

13. For a thorough theatrical discussion of the play, see Tonelli, *Sophocles' "Oedipus" and the Tale of the Theater*.

14. Hubert, "L'Anti-Oedipe de Corneille."

15. *Webster's Third New International Dictionary of the English Language*, s.v. "play." Tonelli and Hubert, "Theatricality: The Burden of the Text."

16. Reprinted in Donald Stone's *Four Renaissance Tragedies*.

17. Susan Snyder in *The Comic Matrix of Shakespeare's Tragedies* has provided illuminating commentaries on the function of comic structures in Shakespearean tragedy.

18. Critics quoted in the following chapters.

19. A study by Vivian Thomas, *The Moral Universe of Shakespeare's Problem Plays*, testifies to the fact that traditional mimetic approaches, based on historical research as well as on ethical and social considerations, continue to yield valuable results, all of which goes to show that most methods remain healthy whether fashionable or not. The same holds true for an even more recent study: John D. Cox's remarkably erudite *Shakespeare and the Dramaturgy of Power*. The dramaturgy featured in the title differs markedly from theatricality and performance.

20. Calderwood does this most notably in *To Be and Not to Be*.

2. Verbal Choreography and Metaphorical Space in *Much Ado about Nothing*

1. See Jorgensen, *Redeeming Shakespeare's Words*, pp. 24–42, for a discussion of the theological playfulness and ambiguity of the term. See also Goddard, *The Meaning of Shakespeare*, for a discussion of the word as the

realm of pure possibility and artistic creation: the power of nothing (p. 97). See in addition Horowitz, "Imagining the Real," for the connection between perception and "noting."

2. For the pun on musical notation see, in additition to Jorgensen, James J. Wey, "To Grace Harmony," pp. 80–88. We owe to George Kittredge the discovery of this notable pun.

3. "Yet all the feet whereon these measures go / Are only spondees, solemn, grave and slow"; [courantes] "That on a triple dactyl foot do run"; [lavolta] "An anapest is all their music's song / Whose first two feet are short and third is long" (Davies, *Orchestra*, p. 31, stanza 66; p. 32, stanzas 69, 70).

4. Notably, Storey, "The Success of *Much Ado about Nothing*" and William G. McCollom, "The Role of Wit in *Much Ado about Nothing*," pp. 67–80. Tommy Ruth Waldo in *Musical Terms as Rhetoric* provides a searching analysis of ambiguity in connection with musical terminology.

5. See in this connection Brissenden, *Shakespeare and the Dance.*

6. Dolmetsche, *Dances of England and France.*

7. "Their [Starry wheels] do a music frame / And they themselves still dance unto the same." Davies also associates speech with dance: "For all the words that from your lips repair / Are nought but tricks and turnings of the air"; the latter probably contains a pun on musical "air" (Davies, *Orchestra*, p. 19, stanza 19; p. 25, stanza 44).

8. "Behold the world, how it is whirled around! / And for it is so whirl'd is named so" (ibid., p. 23, stanza 34).

9. Many scholars insist that Beatrice and Benedick have fallen in love even before the beginning of the play, notably J. Dennis Huston in his *Shakespeare's Comedies of Play*, p. 138. In connection with displacement, gamemanship, and permutation, see Rossiter, "*Much Ado about Nothing*," pp. 47–57.

10. Bertrand Evans in his *Shakespeare's Comedies,* considers with good reason Claudio's brutal treatment of Hero "one of the most poignant scenes in Shakespearean comedy" (p. 81). As such, it may very well provide an extreme and highly pathetic example of hyperbole while relating contrapuntally, but nonetheless affectively, to the lighter moments of gulling that preceded it.

11. Dolmetsche, *Dances of England and France.*

12. The play as a whole makes inordinate use of dilation in the terms of Parker's rhetorical treatment of the subject in "'Dilation' and 'Delation' in *Othello*."

13. Evans, in *Shakespeare's Comedies,* has shown the susceptibility of practicers, in the sense of schemers, to become victims of gulling: "No crowd

of characters in a Shakesperian world exhibits more universal predilection for the game, such readiness to exchange and then exchange again the roles of deceiver and deceived" (p. 69). This exchange of roles suggests the permutations involved in dancing.

14. Huston, in *Shakespeare's Comedies of Play,* says, "this second scene of trickery seems almost a mechanical repetition of the first" (p. 139).

15. For the high esteem in which Renaissance England held rhetoric, for its creative force and its beneficial effects, see Arthur F. Kinney's remarkable study *Humanist Poetics,* notably pp. 3–56.

16. Bouchet d'Ambillou, *Sidère,* fol. 127

3. Music and Framing in *Twelfth Night*

1. See in this connection Manlove, *The Gap in Shakespeare,* for a most perceptive discussion of synesthesia and other forms of interpenetration from a psychological and mimetic standpoint in *Twelfth Night:* "Throughout the play, too, there is emphasis on dislocation, physical and mental" (p. 59). He has also pointed to partial anagrams in names (p. 35), whereby interpenetration begins with the listing of characters. Alexander Leggat in his remarkable *Shakespeare's Comedy of Love* has discussed spatial separation in the play in terms of language. In keeping with his title he concerns himself more with the psychological relationships among the characters than with theatrical performance—for instance, "Malvolio in his dark room is the play's most vivid image of the trapped, isolated self" (p. 244). John W. Draper has provided a most thorough and perceptive study of the comedy: *The "Twelfth Night" of Shakespeare's Audience.*

2. Booth, "*Twelfth Night:* I.1.: The Audience as Malvolio," p. 162.

3. Ibid.

4. Ibid.

5. For an account of the comic possibilities of Olivia's behavior, see ibid., p. 162.

6. In this connection, Manlove states, "In Sir Toby Belch, the shutting in of the self that we see in Olivia and Orsino is turned upside-down." Moreover, he contrasts two kinds of excess in Malvolio and Sir Toby: "excessive isolation from the world and excessive exposure" (*Gap in Shakespeare,* pp. 32, 33).

7. For a brilliant deconstructive analysis of this passage, see Hartman, "Shakespeare's Poetical Character in *Twelfth Night,*" p. 44. According to Slater, *Shakespeare the Director,* "Sir Andrews' barren courtship (which has no source) ironically mirrors Orsino's self-deceiving infatuation" (p. 90).

8. See Manlove, *Gap in Shakespeare,* p. 32, for the connection between Sebastian's activity and the mobility of the sea.

9. Hartman in particular, in "Shakespeare's Poetical Character," has stressed the dominance of language throughout the play.

10. As Manlove has shown in *Gap in Shakespeare,* Sir Toby devotes much of his energy to exposing others, Malvolio in particular (p. 33).

11. Notably in the Prologue to *The Life of King Henry the Fifth.*

12. For a discussion of epiphany, see Hartman, "Shakespeare's Poetical Character," p. 51. Maurice Charney has provided an illuminating account of the festive aspects of the comedy in "Comic Premises of *Twelfth Night,*" pp. 151–65.

13. Booth, *Twelfth Night,* p. 167.

4. Performative Staging in *Measure for Measure*

1. Heraud, *Shakespeare: His Inner Life,* pp. 280–292. Schreiner, "Providential Improvisation in *Measure for Measure,*" pp. 226–36.

2. Knight, "*Measure for Measure* and the Gospels," pp. 27–49.

3. See in this connection Miles, *The Problem of "Measure for Measure,"* p. 208.

4. Pompey and his companions, as R. A. Foakes has shown, represent "vitality, a zest for life" (*Shakespeare: From Satire to Celebration,* p. 18). Pompey, however, like Claudio, shows "the inadequacies of being absolute for life" as Isabella and Angelo reveal "the limitations of being absolute for death" (p. 24).

5. For greater precision in such matters, see the interesting commentary by Darryl J. Gless, "*Measure for Measure*": *The Law and the Convent.*

6. Miles, *The Problem of "Measure for Measure,"* p. 179.

7. Foakes has pointed out the importance of Barnardine in the play, in *Shakespeare,* pp. 25–26.

8. Manlove interprets Isabella's transformation in intellectual rather than theatrical terms: "It is only when she makes the issue one of a contrast between earthly justice and heavenly mercy that she begins to catch fire" (*Gap in Shakespeare,* p. 57).

9. Empson, *The Structure of Complex Words,* pp. 270–84.

10. Slater, in *Shakespeare the Director,* has pointed out the theatrical and symbolic importance of kneeling here and in the closing scene (pp. 74–76).

11. For a remarkable discussion of this passage, see ibid., p. 70.

12. Slater has discussed the duke's soliloquy from the standpoint of the theme of reputation, subordinated to that of the dangers of judgment, (ibid., pp. 151–52).

13. Slater has discussed their positions in terms of staging (ibid., pp. 42–43).

14. See Miles, *The Problem of "Measure for Measure,"* pp. 198–209.

15. As Slater has shown in *Shakespeare the Director,* p. 42.

16. Thomas, *Moral Universe,* p. 186.

17. John D. Cox, in relating various religious and legal aspects of *Measure for Measure* to medieval theater, insists on the shortcomings of Vincentio as a Christ figure: "while the Duke undoubtedly shares with the medieval Christ some functions of divine sovereignty, he is far from godlike and seems an ambigious example at best of the Renaissance commonplace that the king represents God on earth; indeed, in this respect, he is like Shakespeare's English kings," (*Shakespeare and the Dramaturgy,* p. 167). As Cox insists that Vincentio favors the new law (of mercy) as opposed to the old, advocated by Angelo (p. 165), his appreciation of the duke's behavior would seem to confirm that the dramatist has deliberately and systematically reduced to performative and secular terms biblical and other religious allusions repeated throughout the play and appearing initially in the title. Whatever else we may say of Shakespeare's political, legal, or theological intent, he has constrained religion to serve an impressively theatrical purpose.

5. Narratives of Treachery in *Othello*

1. See in this respect Matteo, *Shakespeare's "Othello,"* in particular his discussion of how defenders of Shakespeare reluctantly accepted many of Thomas Rhymer's disparaging comments on the play (pp. 85ff).

2. Bayley, *Shakespeare and Tragedy,* "Her [Desdemona's] unchanging and undiscriminating love restores the balance between the comic and the tragic and sustains the whole precarious structure" (p. 219). See also Snyder, *Comic Matrix of Shakespeare's Tragedies,* p. 74.

3. The storm has also caused a thematically important delay in Othello's and Desdemona's plans or, as Patricia Parker puts it in "'Dilation' and 'Delation' in *Othello,*" pp. 62 and 64–65, a dilation, involving not only a loss of time but also a revelation, amplification, and even delation. It would thus appear that the storm moves inward and reverses itself while maintaining its intensity on a rhetorical level.

4. In other respects, one might follow Bernard Spivack's lead in *Shakespeare and the Allegory of Evil,* pp. 56–59, and read the tragedy in terms of a morality play with Iago preempting the part of Vice. This approach has the great advantage, from a performative point of view, of reducing the importance of motivation in Iago's behavior.

5. Manlove has ably discussed jealousy in both Othello and Iago, *Gap in Shakespeare,* pp. 62ff. The Moor may suffer, however, from insecurity con-

cerning his position and appearance as spectacle. But can we consider such insecurity a vice? In any case, it coincides, just like any other psychological weakness, with performative failure.

6. Bergson, *Le Rire*, p. 53ff.

7. Slater among others has associated devil imagery with Iago (*Shakespeare the Director*, pp. 49–50).

8. Rubinstein, *Dictionary of Shakespeare's Sexual Puns*, pp. 11–12.

9. *Le More de Venise*, first performed on October 24, 1829, received considerable applause in spite of the derisive laughter of the classicists. See *Histoire des spectacles*. Vigny admired the diversity of styles in the play: "un style familier, comique, tragique et parfois épique" (*Histoire des spectacles*, p. 848).

10. See Knight, *The Wheel of Fire*, pp. 113–14, and Heilman, *Action and Language in "Othello."* I have frequently relied on Heilman's pertinent remarks concerning, for instance, the Moor's wooing of Desdemona—"he singularly reminds us of an actor falling in love with his audience" (p. 140)—and the villain's stylistic approach—"Iago also pursues his conquest of humanity by a rich vocabulary of the base, the inhuman, and the subhuman" (p. 110).

11. E. A. J. Honigmann has described Othello's language as "more dangerously inflated than that of any other Shakespearean tragic hero" ("Shakespeare's Bombast," p. 159). It would seem that *Othello*, as a theatrical score, relies on inflated rhetoric in several registers.

12. In the several senses given to that term by Parker, "'Dilation' and 'Delation' in *Othello*."

13. According to Parker, Iago is the unsurpassed "spectator ab extra, Shakespeare's most wickedly gifted director-cum-author surrogate" (ibid., p. 29).

14. Slater has revealed in *Shakespeare the Director*, p. 99, in connection with the murder of Desdemona, the limitations of the Moor's "mistaken ideal" in matters involving justice.

15. It would seem that Othello practices only too well the art of dilation and delation, so well defined by Parker, "'Dilation' and 'Delation' in *Othello*."

16. Bergson *Le Rire*, pp. 61–68, discusses the snow-ball effect.

17. Slater has identified the circumcisèd dog with Othello himself (*Shakespeare the Director*, p. 99).

18. Dubu, "Le Mouchoir des dames," pp. 269–82.

6. Hamlet: Actor, Student Prince, and Avenger

1. Information derived from the Pelican edition of *Complete Works of Shakespeare*, p. 31.

2. Draper, *The "Hamlet" of Shakespeare's Audience,* p. 195.

3. See Calderwood, *To Be and Not To Be,* for Shakespeare's gamemanship in this respect, notably p. 172. Weimann has provided a valuable deconstructive study of the gap between discursive and nondiscursive activity in his "Mimesis in *Hamlet,*" pp. 275 ff. Manlove has persuasively discussed this gap in terms of communication *(Gap in Shakespeare,* pp. 37–50).

4. See Yves Bonnefoy's note to this effect in his remarkable translation of *Hamlet,* pp. 217–18.

5. For a discussion of delay, see Calderwood, *To Be or Not To Be,* pp. 14 ff. and pp. 23 ff. William Empson has commented on *Hamlet*'s antiquated revenge play structure in "*Hamlet* When New," pp. 15–42. In her article "*Hamlet:* Letters and Spirits," Margaret W. Ferguson has called attention to Hamlet's use of "language to effect a divorce between words and their conventional meanings" (p. 292 ff.). It would seem, therefore, that his delaying tactics affect not only the time of action but also semantics.

6. Calderwood, *To Be or Not To Be,* pp. 123 ff. and 155 ff., has provided a valuable account of messengers and other go-betweens, most of whom function as perpetrators of indirection.

7. For the lack of causal relationships in the plot, see ibid., pp. 150–57. Moreover, Terence Hawkes, in "Telmah," pp. 310–32, has insisted on the recursive as opposed to the linear unfolding of the play.

8. For the ambiguity or "undecidability" in the prince's advice to Gertrude, see Calderwood, *To Be or Not To Be,* p. 54.

9. See Calderwood, *Shakespearean Metadrama,* for discussions of kings as dramatists.

10. Slater sees Hamlet as a theoretician *(Shakespeare the Director,* p. 23). Thus the hero's persistent textual bias would not necessarily preclude disillusionment with an idealistic worldview derived from education.

11. Alexander, in *Poison, Play, and Duel,* shows how Hamlet uses "Remember thee" as a trigger word in applying Quintillian's art of memory to his predicament.

12. Baldwin, *Small Latine and Lesse Greeke* 2:603 ff.

13. Ibid., 2:69 ff.

14. Shakespeare, *Shakespeare's Plays in Quarto,* p. 592.

15. I agree with Empson who, in "*Hamlet* When New" considers the originating plot "antiquated" and, though by no means ridiculous, an overdue target for parody.

16. Alexander, *Poison, Play, and Duel,* p. 14. In this connection, Slater points to Hamlet's use of literary pastiche in his levity toward the ghost and in his behavior in Ophelia's grave *(Shakespeare the Director,* p. 37).

17. See Draper, *The "Hamlet" of Shakespeare's Audience,* pp. 17ff., for Hamlet's relationship with his fellow students.

18. For additional fathers, see Calderwood, *To Be or Not To Be,* p. 18.

19. For the in-joke I am indebted to *Hamlet,* The Players' Shakespeare, p. 188.

20. See Reiss, *Tragedy and Truth,* pp. 162–82.

21. Weimann, in "Mimesis in *Hamlet,*" has provided a thorough discussion of the relationship between performance and representation.

22. Alexander, *Poison, Play, and Duel,* p. 19; Calderwood, *To Be or Not To Be,* p. 182.

23. See Fisch, *Hamlet and the Word,* pp. 37ff.

7. Bridging the Fictional Gap in *The Winter's Tale*

1. See Charles Frey's comments on the ambiguity of the title in *Shakespeare's Vast Romance,* pp. 114–15. In this connection, Foakes has commented: "the world of the play seems governed by chance and coincidence," (*Shakespeare,* p. 127). Chance and coincidence belong usually to the world of the novel rather than to that of drama.

2. Shakespeare has observed the unities in *The Comedy of Errors,* adapted from Plautus; and in *The Taming of the Shrew,* if we view the taming as a play within the play; and in several other comedies, notably *A Midsummer Night's Dream, Twelfth Night,* and *Much Ado about Nothing,* he comes very close to abiding by this classical rule. His treatment of the sixteen-year gap in *The Winter's Tale* appears even more remarkable when we compare his romance to two French adaptations of *Pandosto:* Puget de La Serre, *Pandoste,* (1631) and Alexandre Hardy, *Pandoste* unpublished, both of which required two five-act plays to deal with Greene's short novel.

3. Pyle, *"The Winter's Tale": A Commentary on the Structure,* p. 73. Foakes, who sees Time as the presenter of action, argues that the play does not show the triumph of Time (*Shakespeare,* p. 131).

4. In the glossary of his edition of Shakespeare.

5. Frey, *Shakespeare's Vast Romance,* p. 117.

6. Shakespeare often associates the emergence of a "modern" world with a sense of loss.

7. For the meanings of "grace," a key word, see M. M. Mahood's valuable commentary in "Wordplay in *The Winter's Tale,*" pp. 350–51. Howard Felperin has suggested still another fall from grace, that of language: the "fall into textuality" ("The Deconstruction of Presence in *The Winter's Tale,*" p. 14).

8. Frey stresses the "staged quality" in Leontes' scenes with Hermione

and Paulina, (*Shakespeare's Vast Romance*, p. 134). See also Foakes's comments concerning the distancing of Leontes (*Shakespeare*, pp. 121 and 124).

9. For the performative isolation of the king, see Frey, (*Shakespeare's Vast Romance*, pp. 127ff).

10. Frey has commented on Leontes' "universal mistrust" (ibid., p. 80).

11. Parker, in "'Dilation' and 'Delation' in *Othello*," p. 67, has shown the various implications of the yokel's attainment of a "preposterous estate" (V.ii.139), a malapropism that somehow brings to a climax the numerous reversals that preceded it.

12. "Vivat Mascarillus, fourbum imperator!" (Long live Mascarillus, emperor of rogues!) in Molière's *L'Etourdi.*

13. In appearance but not necessarily in depth. See in this connection Empson, *Some Versions of Pastoral.*

14. Perdita's and Hermione's frankness and forwardness produce contrary effects no doubt because of the generic differences that oppose the two parts.

15. Particularly if we take into account, as does Frey in *Shakespeare's Vast Romance,* the performative aspects of the king's "fixation"; see note 10. As for the rapport between Autolycus and fiction, Anne Barton states that his real association "is with fictions rather than with genuine evil" ("Leontes and the Spider," p. 148).

16. Foakes, who insists on the prevalence of disguise in the second part of the play, stresses Camillo's ability as stage manager and dramatist (*Shakespeare*, pp. 135ff. See also Frey, *Shakespeare's Vast Romance*, p. 132.

17. For an account of performances of *The Winter's Tale* and in particular of the statue scene, see Frey, *Shakespeare's Vast Romance*, pp. 9–48.

18. Robert Greene, *Pandosto*, p. 57.

19. Frey, *Shakespeare's Vast Romance*, p. 95.

20. While Frey reveals the redemptive aspects of the scene (ibid., pp. 158ff.), Pyle stresses its theatricality ("*The Winter's Tale*," pp. 123).

8. The Interplay of Aesthetics and Theatricality

1. Paul Valéry, in "Léonard et les philosophes" 1:1234–69. The epigraph comes from this work, p. 1255.

2. For the new as opposed to the old law, see Cox, *Shakespeare*, pp. 150–71.

3. A term often used by Bergson.

4. Eliot, "Hamlet and His Problems," in *Selected Essays: 1917–1932.*

5. Burke, "*Othello*: An Essay to Illustrate a Method," p. 179.

WORKS CITED

Alexander, Nigel. *Poison, Play, and Duel*. Lincoln: University of Nebraska Press, 1971.

Baldwin, T. W. *Smalle Latine and Lesse Greeke*, 2 vols. Urbana: University of Illinois Press, 1945.

Barton, Anne. "Leontes and the Spider: Language and the Speaker." In *Shakespeare's Styles: Essays in Honour of Kenneth Muir*, edited by Philip Edwards, Inga-Stina Ewbank, and G. K. Hunter. Cambridge: Cambridge University Press, 1980.

Bayley, John. *Shakespeare and Tragedy*. London: Routledge & Kegan Paul, 1981.

Bergson, Henri. *Les Données immédiates de la conscience*. Paris: PUF, 1946.

———. *L'Evolution créatrice*. Paris: PUF, 1983.

———. *Le Rire*. Paris: Quadrige/PUF, 1983.

Bonnefoy, Yves, trans. *Hamlet / Le Roi Lear*. Paris: NRF/Folio, 1978.

Booth, Stephen. "Twelfth Night, I.i. : The Audience as Malvolio." In *Shakespeare's "Rough Magic": Renaissance Essays in Honor of C. L. Barber,* edited by Peter Erickson and Coppelia Kahn. Newark: University of Delaware Press, 1985.

Bouchet d'Ambillou, René. *Sidère, Pastorelle*. Paris: Robert Estienne, 1609.

Brissenden, Alan. *Shakespeare and the Dance,* Atlantic Highlands, N.J.: Humanities Press, 1981.

Brooks, Cleanth. *The Well-Wrought Urn*. New York: Harcourt Brace, 1947.

Burke, Kenneth. *A Grammar of Motives*. Berkeley and Los Angeles: University of California Press, 1969.

———. "*Othello:* An Essay to illustrate a Method," *Hudson Review* 4 (Summer 1951): 165–203.

Calderwood, James L. *Shakespearean Metadrama*. Minneapolis: University of Minnesota Press, 1971.

———. *To Be and Not to Be: Negation and Metadrama in "Hamlet."* New York: Columbia University Press, 1983.

Charney, Maurice. "Comic Premises of *Twelfth Night.*" In *Comedy: New Perspectives*, special issue of *New York Literary Forum*, Spring 1978, pp. 151–65.

Cocteau, Jean. *The Infernal Machine and Other Plays*. New York: New Directions, 1967.

Cox, John D. *Shakespeare and the Dramaturgy of Power*. Princeton: Princeton University Press, 1989.

Davies, Sir John. *Orchestra or a Poem of Dancing*, Edited by E. M. W. Tillyard. London: Chatto & Windus, 1947.

Derrida, Jacques. *Derrida and* Différance. Edited by David Wood and Robert Bernaconi. Evanston, Ill.: Northwestern University Press, 1988.

———. "La Différance." In *Tel Quel—Théorie d'ensemble*. Paris: Editions du Seuil, 1968.

Dolmetsche, Mabel. *Dances of England and France*. London: Routledge & Kegan Paul, 1959.

Draper, John W. *The "Hamlet" of Shakespeare's Audience*. New York: Octagon Books, 1966.

———. *The "Twelfth Night" of Shakespeare's Audience*. New York: Octagon Books, 1975.

Dubu, Jean. "Le Mouchoir des dames." In *Mélanges à la mémoire de Franco Simone*. Genève: Slatkine, 1983.

Eliot, T. S., *Selected Essays: 1917–1932*. New York: Harcourt Brace, 1932.

Empson, William. "*Hamlet* When New." *Sewanee Review* 41 (1953): 15–42.

———. *Some Versions of Pastoral*. Norfolk: New Directions, 1960.

———. *The Structure of Complex Words*. London: Chatto & Windus, 1951.

Evans, Bertrand. *Shakespeare's Comedies*. Oxford: Clarendon Press, 1960.

Felperin, Howard. "The Deconstruction of Presence in *The Winter's Tale.*" In *Shakespeare and the Question of Theory*. London: Routledge, Chapman & Hall, 1985.

Ferguson, Margaret W. "*Hamlet*: Letters and Spirits." In *Shakespeare and the Question of Theory*. London: Routledge, Chapman & Hall, 1985.

Fisch, Harold. *Hamlet and the Word*. New York: Ungar, 1971.

Foakes, R. A. *Shakespeare, the Dark Comedies to the Last Plays: From Satire to Celebration*. Charlottesville: University Press of Virginia, 1971.

Frey, Charles. *Shakespeare's Vast Romance: A Study of "The Winter's Tale."* Columbia: University of Missouri Press, 1980.

Gless, Darryl J. *"Measure for Measure": The Law and the Convent.* Princeton: Princeton University Press, 1979.

Goddard, Harold P. *The Meaning of Shakespeare.* 2 vols. Chicago: Chicago University Press, 1951.

Greene, Robert. *Pandosto: The Triumph of Time.* New York: Duffield & Company, 1907.

Hartman, Geoffrey H. "Shakespeare's Poetical Character in *"Twelfth Night."* In *Shakespeare and the Question of Theory.* London: Routledge, Chapman & Hall, 1985.

Hartman, Geoffrey H., and Patricia Parker, eds. *Shakespeare and the Question of Theory.* London: Routledge, Chapman & Hall, 1985.

Hawkes, Terence. "Telmah." In *Shakespeare and the Question of Theory.* London: Routledge, Chapman & Hall, 1985.

Heilman, Robert B. *Action and Language in "Othello."* Lexington: University of Kentucky Press, 1956.

Heraud, John A. *Shakespere: His Inner Life as Intimated in his Works.* London: Maxwell, 1865.

Histoire des spectacles. Edited by Guy Dumur. Vol. 19 of *Encyclopédie de la Pleiade.* Paris: NRF, 1965.

Honigmann, E. A. J. "Shakespeare's Bombast." In *Shakespeare's Styles: Essays in Honour of Kenneth Muir,* edited by Philip Edwards, Inga-Stina Ewbank, and G . K. Hunter. Cambridge: Cambridge University Press, 1980.

Horowitz, David. "Imagining the Real." In *Twentieth-Century Interpretations of "Much Ado about Nothing,"* edited by Walter R. Davis. Englewood Cliffs, N. J.: Prentice-Hall, 1969.

Hubert, Judd D. "L'Anti-Oedipe" de Corneille." *Revue du Dix-Septième Siècle,"* April, 1985, pp. 47–55.

Huston, J. Dennis. *Shakespeare's Comedies of Play.* New York: Columbia University Press, 1981.

Jonson, Ben. *Volpone.* Edited by Jonas Barish. Arlington Heights, Ill.: AHM, 1958.

Jorgensen, Paul A. *Redeeming Shakespeare's Words.* Berkeley and Los Angeles: University of California Press, 1962.

Kinney, Arthur F. *Humanist Poetics, Thought, Rhetoric, and Fiction in Sixteenth-Century England.* Amherst: University of Massachusetts Press, 1986.

Knight, G. Wilson. "*Measure for Measure* and the Gospels." In *Twentieth-Century Interpretations of "Measure for Measure,"* edited by George L. Geckle. Englewood Cliffs: N. J.: Prentice-Hall, 1970.

———. *The Wheel of Fire*. London: Oxford University Press, 1941.

La Taille, Jean de. *Saül le furieux*. In *Four Renaissance Tragedies*, with an Introduction and Glossary by Donald Stone, Jr. Cambridge: Harvard University Press, 1966.

Leggat, Alexander. *Shakespeare's Comedy of Love*. London: Methuen, 1974.

McCollom, William G. "The Role of Wit" in *Much Ado about Nothing*." In *Twentieth-Century Interpretations of "Much Ado about Nothing*," edited by Walter R. Davis. Englewood Cliffs, N. J.: Prentice-Hall, 1969.

Mahood, M. M. "Wordplay in *The Winter's Tale*." In *Shakespeare's Later Comedies*. Harmondsworth: Penguin Books, 1971.

Manlove, Colin N. *The Gap in Shakespeare*. Totowa, N. J.: Barnes & Noble, 1981.

Matteo, Gino J. *Shakespeare's "Othello: The Study and the Stage 1604–1904*. Salzburg: Institut für Englische Sprache und Literatur, 1974.

Miles, Rosalind. *The Problem of "Measure for Measure*." London: Vision Press, 1976.

Miller, J. Hillis. "The Triumph of Theory, the Resistance to Reading, and the Question of the Material Base." *PMLA* 102 (May 1987): 281–91.

Molière. *Oeuvres complètes*. 3 vols. Paris: Garnier, 1962.

Parker, Patricia. "'Dilation' and 'Delation' in *Othello*." In *Shakespeare and the Question of Theory*. London: Routledge, Chapman & Hall, 1985.

———. *Literary Fat Ladies*. London: Methuen, 1987.

Partridge, Eric. *Origins: A Short Etymological Dictionary of Modern English*. New York: Macmillan, n.d.

Pechter, Edward. "The New Historicism and Its Discontents: Politicizing Renaissance Drama." *PMLA* 102 (May 1987): 292–303.

Puget de La Serre, Jean. *Pandoste ou la princesse malheureuse*. Paris: Billaine, 1631.

Pyle, Fitzroy. *"The Winter's Tale": A Commentary on the Structure*. London: Routledge, 1969.

Reiss, Timothy. *Tragedy and Truth*. New Haven: Yale University Press, 1980.

Rossiter, A. P. "*Much Ado about Nothing*." In *Shakespeare: The Comedies, Twentieth-Century Views*. Englewood Cliffs, N. J.: Prentice-Hall, 1965.

Rubinstein, Frankie. *A Dictionary of Shakespeare's Sexual Puns and Their Significance*. London: Macmillan, 1984.

Schreiner, Louise. "Providential Improvisation in *Measure for Measure*." *PMLA* 97 (March, 1982): 226–36.

Shakespeare. *The Complete Works*. Edited by George Lyman Kittredge. Boston: Ginn & Company, 1936.

———. *The Complete Works*. The Pelican Shakespeare; General Editor, Alfred Harbage. New York: The Viking Press, 1979.

———. *Hamlet*. The Players' Shakespeare series, edited by J. H. Walter. London: Heinemann, 1978).

———. *Shakespeare's Plays in Quarto*. Berkeley and Los Angeles: University of California Press, 1981.

Slater, Ann Pasternak. *Shakespeare the Director*. Totowa, N. J.: Barnes & Noble, 1982.

Snyder, Susan. *The Comic Matrix of Shakespeare's Tragedies*. Princeton: Princeton University Press, 1979.

Spivak, Bernard. *Shakespeare and the Allegory of Evil: The History of a Metaphor in Relation to His Major Villains*. New York: Columbia University Press, 1958.

Stone, Donald. *Four Renaissance Tragedies*. Cambridge: Harvard University Press, 1966.

Storey, Graham. "The Success of *Much Ado about Nothing*." In *Twentieth-Century Interpretations of "Much Ado about Nothing."* Englewood Cliffs, N. J.: Prentice-Hall, 1969.

Thomas, Vivian. *The Moral Universe of Shakespeare's Problem Plays*. London: Croom Helm, 1987.

Tonelli, Franco. *Sophocles' "Oedipus" and the Tale of the Theater*. Ravenna: Longo Editore, 1983.

Tonelli, Franco and Hubert, Judd D. "Theatricality: The Burden of the Text." *Sub-Stance* 21 (1978): 79–102.

Valéry, Paul. "Léonard et les philosophes." In *Oeuvres complètes*. Vol. 2. Paris: NRF, 1958.

Waldo, Tommy Ruth. *Musical Terms as Rhetoric: The Complexity of Shakespeare's Dramatic Style*. Salzburg: Salzburg Studies in English Literature, 1974.

Weimann, Robert. "Mimesis in *Hamlet*." In *Shakespeare and the Question of Theory*. London: Routledge, Chapman & Hall, 1985.

———. "Shakespeare (De)Canonized: Conflicting Uses of 'Authority' and Representation." *NLH* 20 (Autumn 1988): 65–81.

Wey, James J. "To Grace Harmony: Musical Design in *Much Ado about Nothing*." In *Twentieth-Century Interpretations of "Much Ado about Nothing*," edited by Walter R. Davis. Englewood Cliffs, N. J.: Prentice-Hall, 1969.

INDEX

This is an index of the writers considered in this book. The subentries indicate topics on which the writers' views are discussed.